Gary E. McCuen

IDEAS IN CONFLICT SERIES

502 Second Street
Hudson, Wisconsin 54016
Phone (715) 386-7113

Library of Congress Cataloging-in-Publication Data

McCuen, Gary E.
  The religious right.

  (Ideas in conflict)
  Bibliography: p.
  Summary: A collection of essays which define "the religious right", discussing their attitudes regarding foreign policy, economic and social justice, homosexuality, and AIDS, from differing viewpoints. Includes a section on televangelists.
  1. Evangelicalism—United States.—Controversial literature. 2. Fundamentalism—Controversial literature. 3. Conservatism—United States—Controversial literature. 4. Christianity and politics. 5. United States—Politics and government—1981-   . 6. United States—Church history—20th century. [1. Evangelicalism. 2. Christianity and politics] I. Title. II. Series: Ideas in conflict series.
  BR1642.U5M27 1989   320.5′5′0973   87-43346
  ISBN 0-86596-068-2

Illustration & photo credits

American Lutheran Church 187, Don Carlton 73, Christian 166, Christian Broadcasting Network 130, *Conservative Digest* 23, Susan Harlan 18, 96, Mary Harrison 156, Steve Kelley 82, Henry Martin 149, Eleanor Mill 117, 191, Steve Sack 29, William Sanders 43, 137, David Seavey 124, *Sequoia* 101, Carol ★ Simpson 102, 172, Ron Swanson 50.

© 1989 by Gary E. McCuen Publications, Inc.
502 Second Street • Hudson, Wisconsin 54016
    (715) 386-7113
publications inc. International Standard Book Number 0-86596-068-2
Printed in the United States of America

CONTENTS

CHAPTER 3 THE TELEVANGELISTS

CHAPTER 4 ECONOMIC AND SOCIAL JUSTICE

CHAPTER 5 RELIGION, AIDS, AND HOMOSEXUALITY

REASONING SKILL DEVELOPMENT

These activities may be used as individualized study guides for students in libraries and resource centers or as discussion catalysts in small group and classroom discussions.

IDEAS in CONFLICT ®

This series features ideas in conflict on political, social, and moral issues. It presents counterpoints, debates, opinions, commentary, and analysis for use in libraries and classrooms. Each title in the series uses one or more of the following basic elements:

Introductions that present an issue overview giving historic background and/or a description of the controversy.

Counterpoints and debates carefully chosen from publications, books, and position papers on the political right and left to help librarians and teachers respond to requests that treatment of public issues be fair and balanced.

Symposiums and forums that go beyond debates that can polarize and oversimplify. These present commentary from across the political spectrum that reflect how complex issues attract many shades of opinion.

A *global* emphasis with foreign perspectives and surveys on various moral questions and political issues that will help readers to place subject matter in a less culture-bound and ethnocentric frame of reference. In an ever-shrinking and interdependent world, understanding and cooperation are essential. Many issues are global in nature and can be effectively dealt with only by common efforts and international understanding.

Reasoning skill study guides and discussion activities provide ready-made tools for helping with critical reading and evaluation of content. The guides and activities deal with one or more of the following:

RECOGNIZING AUTHOR'S POINT OF VIEW

INTERPRETING EDITORIAL CARTOONS

VALUES IN CONFLICT

WHAT IS EDITORIAL BIAS?

WHAT IS SEX BIAS?

WHAT IS POLITICAL BIAS?

WHAT IS ETHNOCENTRIC BIAS?

WHAT IS RACE BIAS?

WHAT IS RELIGIOUS BIAS?

From across **the political spectrum** *varied sources are presented for research projects and classroom discussions. Diverse opinions in the series come from magazines, newspapers, syndicated columnists, books, political speeches, foreign nations, and position papers by corporations and nonprofit institutions.*

About the Editor

Gary E. McCuen is an editor and publisher of anthologies for public libraries and curriculum materials for schools. Over the past 18 years his publications of over 200 titles have specialized in social, moral, and political conflict. They include books, pamphlets, cassettes, tabloids, filmstrips, and simulation games, many of them designed from his curriculums during 11 years of teaching junior and senior high school social studies. At present he is the editor and publisher of the *Ideas in Conflict* series and the *Editorial Forum* series.

CHAPTER 1

DEFINING THE RELIGIOUS RIGHT
Ideas in Conflict

INTRODUCTION

Chapter one attempts to define the Religious Right as a whole but, as in all groups, the whole is composed of many parts. This brief introduction serves to define the various movements within the Religious Right and to assist you in your reading.

Evangelicals is an "umbrella" term used to describe people that emphasize the absolute authority of the Bible and believe in converting others to their brand of Christianity. Evangelicals can be either fundamentalist, charismatic, or pentacostal. These terms are defined below.

- **Fundamentalists** believe in a literal interpretation of the Bible and apply that interpretation to everyday matters. They also stress personal salvation and tend to be critical of charismatics and of people whose views are non-evangelical.

- **Charismatics** stress the intimate workings of the Holy Spirit, such as faith healing (the ability to perform healing miracles) and speaking in tongues (a state of fervent prayer in which people utter strings of unintelligible syllables considered to have deep spiritual significance).

- **Pentacostals** also believe in faith healing and stress the Holy Spirit's work but, unlike charismatics, they avoid public display of such charismatic gifts.

- **Born-again Christians** are people who have found new life in Jesus and could belong in any of the above categories.

DEFINING THE RELIGIOUS RIGHT

THE MORAL MAJORITY

Jerry Falwell

The Reverend Jerry Falwell is the founder of the 21,000-member Thomas Road Baptist Church in Lynchburg, Virginia. His weekly television program, "The Old-Time Gospel Hour," is seen on over 300 stations. In 1979, Falwell organized the Washington-based Moral Majority, Inc., a non-profit organization intended to counter political liberalism and focused on education, lobbying, endorsement of political candidates, and legal aid. Falwell served as the Moral Majority's president until his resignation in November 1987.

Points to Consider:

1. Why does Falwell believe that America's grand old flag is "going down the drain"?
2. Describe the four "burning crises" we are facing in the Decade of Destiny.
3. What is the Congressional Petition on Moral Issues and what does Falwell plan to do with it?
4. How would you respond to Falwell's letter?

Reprinted from a 1987 public letter written by Moral Majority founder, Jerry Falwell. The letter and accompanying Congressional petition explain who the Moral Majority is and the organization's purpose.

I believe that the overwhelming majority of Americans are sick and tired of the way the amoral liberals are trying to corrupt our nation from its commitment to freedom, democracy, traditional morality, and the free enterprise system.

*Is Our
Grand Old Flag
Going Down
The Drain?*

Dear Friend,

I have bad news for you:
The answer to the question above is "YES"!
Our grand old flag is going down the drain. Don't kid yourself. You may wake up some morning and discover that Old Glory is no longer waving freely.
Just look at what's happening here in America:
—Known practicing homosexual teachers have invaded the classrooms, and the pulpits of our churches.
—Smut peddlers sell their pornographic books—under the protection of the courts!
—And X-rated movies are allowed in almost every community because there is no legal definition of obscenity.
—Meanwhile, right in our own homes the television screen is full of R-rated movies and sex and violence.
—Believe it or not, we are the first civilized nation in history to legalize abortion—in the late months of pregnancy! Murder!
How long can all this go on?
I repeat: Our grand old flag is going down the drain.
And not just here in America—we have broken our treaty with Taiwan, our best friend in the Orient.
We gave away the Panama Canal, to prevent "offending" a leftist government!
There are some persons in high places—including the National Council of Churches—who would advocate negotiating with the PLO—a terrorist group committed to the annihilation of the State of Israel.
And unless we re-build our military strength and keep a careful watch over the strength of our military position . . .
. . . one day the Russians may be able to pick up the telephone and call Washington, D.C., and dictate the terms of our surrender.
And when that happens—Old Glory is down the drain, forever.
Is God finished with America? I don't believe He is. My reasons for being optimistic about America are:

11

BEWARE OF SOVIETS

"While we are working and praying towards a spiritual awakening in this country, at the same time we mustn't be foolish or naive about the intentions of the Soviets. Their goal has been, and is now, world conquest."

—Jerry Falwell

USA Today, *December 30, 1983.*

1. America has more God-fearing citizens per capita than any other nation on earth.
2. America is the only major world power supporting the nation of Israel today. God promised Abraham in Genesis 12:3 "And I will bless them that bless thee, and curse them that curseth thee." God has blessed America because America has blessed the Jew—His chosen people. Israel also has a legal and historical right to the land of Palestine.
3. America is the last hope for the free world today.

But time is short: and this is why I am writing this letter to you.

I believe that the overwhelming majority of Americans are sick and tired of the way the amoral liberals are trying to corrupt our nation from its commitment to freedom, democracy, traditional morality, and the free enterprise system.

And I believe that the majority of Americans agree on the basic moral values which this nation was founded upon over 200 years ago.

Today we face four burning crises as we continue in this Decade of Destiny—the 1980s—loss of our freedom by giving in to the Communists; the destruction of the family unit; the deterioration of the free enterprise system; and the crumbling of basic moral principles which has resulted in the legalizing of abortion, wide-spread pornography, and a drug problem of epidemic proportions.

That is why I went to Washington, D.C. in June of 1979, and started a new organization—

The Moral Majority

And if you agree with me that our grand old flag is going down the drain, I invite you to join with me in this fight to save America.

Right now you may be wondering: "But I thought Jerry Falwell was the preacher on the 'Old-Time Gospel Hour' television program?"

You are right. For over twenty-four years I have been calling the nation back to God from the pulpit on radio and television.

But in recent months I have been led to do more than just preach—I have been compelled to take action.

I have made the commitment to go right into the halls of Congress and fight for laws that will save America.

But—as a pastor—my hands are tied. I must be very careful when I speak out on certain "moral issues" on my nationally televised program, the "Old-Time Gospel Hour."

Many of these moral issues have now become very political. Abortion, pornography, homosexuality, and the traditional family are now very "hot" political issues.

But how can I be silent about the cancers that are destroying the moral fiber of our nation?

Therefore, I have gone to Washington, D.C.—as a private citizen—rented an office only a few blocks from the nation's capitol, and organized the Moral Majority. I can do this without violating the principle of separation of Church and State. I believe very much in this principle.

I will still be preaching every Sunday on the "Old-Time Gospel Hour"—and I still must be a husband and father to my precious family in Lynchburg, Virginia.

But as God gives me the strength, I must do more. I must go into the halls of Congress and fight for laws that will protect the grand old flag...

...for the sake of our children and grandchildren.

Will you join me in this bold venture? Will you help me save our grand old flag from going down the drain? If your answer is "YES," then I urge you to fill out the enclosed Congressional Petition on Moral Issues.

You will find five questions on:

1. Abortion
2. Pornography
3. Homosexuals
4. School Prayers
5. Military Strength

If you will let me know exactly how you stand on these vital issues, I will take the results of your petition right to the offices of the Congressmen from your state.

The results will speak loud and clear:

"It's about time you started listening to what the grassroots Americans have to say!"

"They are the Moral Majority!"

Believe me, that will get their attention. That was proven beyond question in the last national election.

In fact, nothing gets the attention of your Congressmen more than a message from a person who can vote him or her in (or out!) of office.

Will you send me your Congressional Petition on Moral Issues today?

And will you consider sending along a contribution of $10, $25, or $100? I receive absolutely no salary from the Moral Majority, but I must pay my loyal staff.

And the Moral Majority Report newspaper and radio commentaries must be paid for. Operation costs must be underwritten also.

Your gifts are not tax-deductible—but time is running out for America—and I believe you are willing to give up a tax deduction in order to turn this nation around.

In appreciation for your gift I will send you:

1. Regular copies of our hard-hitting newspaper—Moral Majority Report.

2. Plus—complete information about new bills— of interest to you—as they are introduced to Congress.

May I hear from you? And will you complete your Congressional Petition on Moral Issues? There is only one way to save our grand old flag from going down the drain. We have made tremendous progress in the last few months.

But now the real work is still ahead. I need your help. *The Moral Majority must speak up!* God bless you.

For the sake of America,
Jerry Falwell
Moral Majority

TO THE CONGRESS OF THE UNITED STATES OF AMERICA

**The Undersigned Hereby Petitions Congress
To Pass Laws In Support of My Moral Opinions Listed Below**

1. Are you in favor of your tax dollar being used to support abortion on demand?
   ☐ YES   ☐ NO
2. Do you believe that smut peddlers should be protected by the courts and the Congress, so they can openly sell pornographic materials to your children?
   ☐ YES   ☐ NO
3. Should school systems that receive federal funds be forced to hire known practicing and soliciting homosexual teachers?
   ☐ YES   ☐ NO
4. Do you agree that voluntary prayer should be banned from the public schools?
   ☐ YES   ☐ NO
5. Do you agree with the liberals who say we should not increase our military strength up to the level of the Russians before continuing the Salt Treaty process?
   ☐ YES   ☐ NO

Your Signature Above

14

DEFINING
THE RELIGIOUS RIGHT

THE MORAL MAJORITY
IS NEITHER

Gilbert Padilla

Father Gilbert Padilla wrote this editorial in his capacity as the pastor of Holy Family Church in Tucson, Arizona. His editorial appeared in the National Catholic Reporter, *a liberal, independent Catholic newsweekly.*

Points to Consider:

1. According to the author, how would Jerry Falwell define peace?
2. Explain what the author means when he says fundamentalism is a psychology.
3. How does the author define faith? What evidence does the author provide to demonstrate that fundamentalists lack faith?
4. How do fundamentalists reconcile their religion with oppression and the building of nuclear warheads?

Gilbert Padilla, "The Moral Majority is Neither," *National Catholic Reporter*, November 1, 1985, pp. 15-16. Reprinted by permission of the *National Catholic Reporter*, P.O. Box 419281, Kansas City, MO 64141.

***For Falwell, peace is control of the many by the few
in a worldwide concentration camp because God wills
it.***

Jerry Falwell is known as the leader of the fundamentalist Moral Majority. It is all true, he is the founder and leader, and the Moral Majority is fundamentalist in thought. Falwell's attitude to the movie "The Day After," his ill-worded description of Desmond Tutu, and then his condescending apology to Tutu demonstrate graphically what it means to be a fundamentalist. For Falwell, peace is control of the many by the few in a worldwide concentration camp because God wills it.

Wherever and whenever we find fundamentalism, we see three basic identifying factors come to the surface. These are the lack of scholarship, the lack of faith, and the lack of compassion.

Lack of Scholarship

Fundamentalism is not really a theology, even though we often associate it with people of strong religious belief. It is a psychology. Certain types of people just gravitate to that kind of thinking. It has nothing to do with intelligence. Fundamentalists are not dumb; they might actually be highly intelligent, but they are narrow and limited in vision. It is a psychology of almost complete limitations.

We do not find fundamentalists among the great scientists and theologians of the world. If they were scholars, they would not be fundamentalists. In fact, fundamentalists often scorn higher learning and denounce it. They have locked themselves into an attitude that is unteachable and closed to learning any more or any differently from what they already hold as certain. Ignorance and intelligence can exist in the same person, and they often do. Ignorance is the lack of due knowledge. A person who is smart enough to know something, and who should know this, is ignorant.

There are various types of ignorance. The ignorance so characteristic of the fundamentalist thinking is crass or stubborn ignorance. It is the stubborn refusal to be instructed. It is the ignorance that is cemented into "I don't care, this is the way I think, I will not accept any other and I will stand up in my opinion against anyone." The lack of scholarship common among the fundamentalists reflects itself in the attitude that there is no more to learn. This is the spiritual pride that "God has told me and what God says is it."

There is no higher authority than God, but when we claim a special exclusive communication from God to ourselves that excludes everyone else, that can become suspect. There is pride here, but this is also a cover-up for the uncertainty and fear that occurs at the end of every millennium about the end of the world and the Second Coming of Christ. It is easier to hang on with a tightly clenched fist to what one wants,

MORAL MAJORITY IS ON THE WRONG TRACK

Billy Graham agrees that Moral Majority is on the wrong track, a judgment by the most important evangelist that undoubtedly complicates the task of Reverend Falwell. Graham got hurt by the Watergate scandal and his close connection with and defense of President Nixon. He swears that he has learned to stay away from politics and he now argues that evangelists should be preaching the gospel, not dabbling in politics. Moreover, while Graham too has long been a stern advocate of the more moral America, he complains that Moral Majority has no notion of social morality and thinks that its focus on abortion, sexual morality, and school prayers demonstrates a lack of larger social concern. At the same time, Graham, who was a surprise supporter of the Salt II treaty, complains that Moral Majority is too nationalistic and is under the impression that God has specially anointed the United States, whereas nowadays Graham believes such an idea is in error. God never selects countries, only human souls.

Robert Booth Fowler, Religion and Politics in America, *1985.*

despite evidence to the contrary, than it is to investigate and open oneself up to the challenge of further learning. Insecurity, fear, closed minds, and tight fists are the basis of the fundamentalist persuasion.

Lack of Faith

Fundamentalists claim they have a great faith. It is, rather, a lack of faith. Faith is the science of the unseen. It is the step into the dark. It is assent on the authority of the one who reveals. Fundamentalists do not believe. They have their whole religious structure centered on the printed word, the word they can read and read literally as though the word had dropped out of the sky from heaven written in English.

Seeing and faith cancel each other out. That is the reason for the statement, "No one in heaven believes in God." Thomas the apostle would not believe the testimony of his brothers that Jesus had risen. He claimed he would not believe; he had to have experiential proof. Thomas never did make an act of faith in the resurrected Christ, his act of faith was in the divinity of Christ. It is much the same with the fundamentalists. They demand to see the chapter and the verses and, if it does not say it, they don't accept it. In fact, they have replaced Christ with the printed word.

Illustration by Susan Harlan. Copyright 1986, *USA Today*. Reprinted with permission.

Faith is frightening. It means leaping into the darkness and letting go. It is like venturing out into the deep water with no visible help around. Here is where the fundamentalists show their lack of faith. They demand complete security and tangibility. Their security is the printed word, and they will not venture beyond it, but they render the word a dead word like any other dictionary.

Fundamentalists give evidence of a desperate need of God. But because of their lack of faith and because of their unwillingness to give up their way of life, they channel all their energy into a tunnel vision. This is the reason they can reconcile their religion with making nuclear warheads that will exterminate tens of thousands of people. This they can justify if there is nothing in the printed word that denounces nuclear war. The Bible does not mention nuclear war or nuclear missiles. This could be the reason fundamentalism is so often found among those who work for companies involved in making such weapons. The same applies to the multinational corporations that control the economic destinies of entire populations. There may be injustice and oppression, but they can "search the Scriptures" and not find it mentioned. They are safe.

Lack of Compassion

The lack of faith and spirituality lead to the lack of compassion. The mark of the mystic is compassion, sensitivity to suffering—his own and that of others around the world. Fundamentalists never pray for anyone except themselves or for their own immediate concerns. The oppressed people of other countries never seem to gain their attention. They so easily dismiss as communists people who rise up in protest against their condition, and then they advocate all forms of force to put them down.

This does not mean that all fundamentalists are fanatics, but all fanatics are fundamentalists.

So when Jerry Falwell stands up before the country and, in his smug way, speaks out in favor of the oppressors and against the oppressed and advocates the use of nuclear warfare to insure his way of life by promoting national security in the name of God, then we can certainly say he fulfills the conditions and characteristics of fundamentalism. And we know the truth of the bumper sticker that says, "The Moral Majority is neither."

3

DEFINING
THE RELIGIOUS RIGHT

THE POLITICAL CONTRIBUTIONS
OF THE RELIGIOUS RIGHT

Dinesh D'Souza

Dinesh D'Souza is the former managing editor of Policy Review, *a quarterly publication of the Heritage Foundation—a conservative research center in Washington, D.C. He wrote this article in his capacity as a senior policy analyst for domestic policy at the White House.*

Points to Consider:

1. Describe the difficulties that the New Right and Christian Right have faced in the political arena.
2. What kind of changes have the Religious Right brought about in the past decade? Do you agree or disagree with these changes? Why?
3. How has the Religious Right helped to revive America's founding tradition?
4. Do you think the Religious Right has a strong political future? Why or why not?

Dinesh D'Souza, "Out of the Wilderness: The Political Education of the Christian Right," *Policy Review,* Summer 1987, pp. 54-59. Reprinted with permission from *Policy Review,* Summer 1987. *Policy Review* is the flagship publication of the Heritage Foundation.

At a time when moral issues were totally submerged under a welter of special interest scrambling, the Religious Right came along to invoke the tradition and raise the alarm. The country has responded, and though much remains to be thought about and done, everyone is better off for their coming.

One of the most important reasons for the conservative ascent to power in the last decade is the political contribution of the New Right and the Christian Right. Membership in the Christian Right includes millions of evangelicals and fundamentalists who, ostracized by the mainstream culture for half a century, have returned to the public square to make a bid for political influence and social acceptance. Together with a constellation of New right strategists and organizations fighting the Equal Rights Amendment, abortion on demand, and other liberal programs, the Christian Right provided Ronald Reagan with several million voters and activists. Statistical evidence suggests that President Reagan could not have come to power without their support. Yet the allegiance of these groups to the conservative cause remains fragile, even dubious. In 1988, it will not be surprising if many of these people sit out the elections or at least fail to mobilize their political forces.

Coming out of the Closets

It may be too early to write an epitaph for the New Right and Christian Right. . .The New Right and Christian Right, as newcomers to the political stage, have encountered difficulties accommodating the constraints of pluralistic democracy. They have fared quite well in making allies. They have not been as successful dealing with those with whom they disagree. Their populist strategies have always been Manichean in tone: a battle of good versus evil, light versus darkness. As James Robison, a Religious Right televangelist, barked, "I'm sick and tired of hearing about all the radicals and perverts and liberals and leftists and Communists coming out of the closets. It's time for God's people to come out of the closets, out of the churches, and change America." A National Conservative Political Action Committee (NCPAC) letter informed subscribers, "Your tax dollars are being used to pay for grade school courses that teach your children that cannibalism, wife swapping, and the murder of infants and the elderly are acceptable behavior." Going from such rhetoric to the politics of compromise and barter is an understandably difficult project. And its stridency of tone and biblical invocations disturb many groups, including some Catholics and Jews familiar with the past of these groups.

Few in the New Right and Christian Right understand that, for all their considerable numbers, they are not as strong as their enemies. Though warnings that fundamentalists are about to "destroy the Democratic and Republican parties and rule the United States'' (Americans for Democratic Action) or alternatively "establish a nightmare of religious and political orthodoxy" (American Civil Liberties Union) are simply absurd, some religious conservatives think they have the power attributed to them by their critics. They don't realize that their best hope for change lies in the decentralization, localization, and privatization of power. More ground can be gained by influencing the moral tenor of their home towns and communities than on such presently futile battles at the federal level as a Human Life Amendment and a School Prayer Amendment.

One serious problem the Christian Right faces is that it is seldom able to counter establishment elites and the mainstream culture on rival turf. In the polemical realm, it is frequently outgunned by its opponents. This is not because the religious conservatives are intellectually inept. Rather, it is because they often insist on employing a scriptural line of argument against people who deny the authority of the Bible to resolve the questions under dispute. It does little good to quote the dire injunctions against homosexuality from the book of Leviticus to people who find the Old Testament outdated and irrelevant on that point. To listen to some fundamentalists, one sometimes gets the impression that the argument for marital fidelity depends entirely on acceptance of the literal truth of the story of Jonah and the whale.

Evangelicals would do well to acquaint themselves with the rational Western tradition making the case for their moral beliefs. In a sense this means partially abandoning the crusade against "secular humanism," for much of this tradition is self-consciously humanistic. In a pluralistic democracy it is impossible to resolve questions purely through an appeal to divine revelation. That strategy only appeals to the already converted. Besides, Aristotle and Aquinas can be valuable allies in the war against secularism and hedonism. It is not always wise to adopt the approach recently taken by Roy Jones, vice president of Jerry Falwell's Liberty Federation. Debating the libertarian, Jones allowed his opponent to speciously claim the entire domain of reason to justify his laissez faire morality; indeed Jones went so far as to de-

New Right leaders depicted on the cover of *Conservative Digest* are, left to right, Phyllis Schlafly, Jerry Falwell, Howard Phillips, Richard Viguerie, Sen. Jesse Helms, John T. Dolan, Morton Blackwell, and Paul Weyrich.

nounce Plato and Locke as godless humanists and to speculate whether they were now in the hot place or the cool place.

Addressing Real and Legitimate Concerns

Despite all this, the contribution of the Religious Right over the past decade has been enormous. It is not best measured in terms of specific policy victories. There certainly have been some of those. The Christian Right defeated a District of Columbia ordinance liberalizing sex laws. It successfully pressured TV sponsors and the networks to reduce sex and violence in programming. It helped get local laws passed on issues such as gay rights and parental control of textbook content. The religious conservatives even won a couple of important victories for creationism and against secular humanism in court.

But the real change brought about with the help of this group is that they have brought morality and ethics to the forefront of the political debate. To be sure, ethics was a major factor during the Vietnam War and Watergate. But this was a particular view of ethics, and a fairly narrow one at that. It had little to do with religious or personal morality. But today, a politician is held accountable not only for bugging his opponent's office or not filling out the proper tax form, but also for adultery. Textbook publishers find it controversial to eschew mention of religion. Schools are under fire for abandoning moral education and promoting ethical and cultural relativism. Remedial efforts are under way in public education, even with the support of liberal groups in some cases.

Recently Norman Lear, founder of People for the American Way, told a conference on values education, "For all our alarm, it is clear that the Religious Right is responding to a real hunger in our society. . .a deep-seated yearning for stable values. . . .When they talk of failures in our educational system, the erosion of our moral standards and the waste of young lives, they are addressing real and legitimate concerns." This from a man who once raised the fascist specter to warn against such groups.

Upholding the Founding Fathers' Standards

Although the Religious Right has not adequately addressed the philosophical issues connected with morality such as the relationship between private theology and public virtue, nevertheless in raising those issues it has forced others to examine them more seriously. Richard John Neuhaus of the Center on Religion and Society maintains that the fundamentalists have set off a trip wire alerting wide segments of the intelligentsia and the public sphere. Even when the evangelicals are at their most bellicose, as when Jerry Falwell said "If God spares America, he owes an apology to Sodom and Gomorrah," there can be a prophetic wisdom in their words. Certainly the portentous statistics surrounding the AIDS virus suggest that the idea that decadent lifestyles may elicit this-worldly retribution is not out of the question. True, natural disasters randomly prey on the guilty and the innocent, but that does not by itself prove that nature and nature's God are always and everywhere undiscriminating.

The New Right and Christian Right have also helped to revive America's founding tradition, a fact worth noting on the occasion of the bicentennial of the Constitution. In fact they can be said to uphold the standards of moral virtue that undergird the entire framework of Western civilization going back to the Greeks.

The five most popular books during America's first 150 years were all religious—John Foxe's *Acts and Monuments,* Richard Allestree's *The Whole Duty of Man,* Richard Baxter's *The Poor Man's Family Book,*

Lewis Bayly's *The Practise of Pietie,* and John Bunyan's *Pilgrim's Progress.* The Founding Fathers may have broken politically with their ancestral and colonial past, but they retained its strong current of moral fervor. Even Thomas Jefferson, in his Bill for Proportioning Crimes and Punishments, proposed castration as fitting punishment for sodomy, proving that if the man was not a Puritan, neither was he a libertarian.

Despite the variance of their personal beliefs and behavior, the Framers shared a rough consensus about the role of religion and morality in public life. Washington: "Let us with caution indulge the supposition that morality can be maintained without religion. . . . Reason and experience forbid us to expect that national morality can prevail in exclusion of religious principle." Jefferson: "Can the liberties of a nation be thought secure when we have removed their only firm basis, a conviction in the minds of the people that these liberties are the gift of God? That they are not to be violated but with His wrath? Indeed I tremble for my country when I reflect that God is just."

Here is the irony: these simple people in their powdered hairdos and pink polyester outfits have become the most ardent defenders of the moral grandeur embodied in the Judeo-Christian tradition, a tradition imported to America by the Founding Fathers.

The future of the New Right and the Christian Right remains cloudy and uncertain. Pat Robertson's candidacy for the presidency in 1988 may re-energize the Christian Right, but Robertson also runs the risk of weakening his religious organization by diverting his attention to politics. The recent flaps over Oral Roberts' fundraising techniques and Jim and Tammy Bakker's erotic and exhibitionistic appetites have brought needed criticism against TV evangelists. The effect of that could either be a lasting stigma, or it could help distinguish the honest pastors from the rogues, the wheat from the chaff.

In any case, at a time when moral issues were totally submerged under a welter of special interest scrambling, the Religious Right came along to invoke the tradition and raise the alarm. The country has responded, and though much remains to be thought about and done, everyone is better off for their coming.

4

DEFINING
THE RELIGIOUS RIGHT

THE RELIGIOUS RIGHT:
A PROGRAM OF
INTOLERANCE AND COERCION

Dr. Peggy L. Shriver

Dr. Peggy L. Shriver wrote this article in her capacity as assistant general secretary for the Office of Research and Evaluation of the National Council of Churches in Christ in the U.S.A. The National Council of Churches is an agency through which churches work together to promote social justice and understanding among people in the U.S. and overseas. It represents approximately 32 Protestant and Orthodox denominations with about 42 million members.

Points to Consider:

1. Describe the Religious Right's political agenda.
2. On what issues are the Religious Right easily manipulated?
3. Why does the author consider military strength the most dangerous attitude of the Religious Right?
4. Do all evangelicals share in the Religious Right's political activism?

Dr. Peggy Shriver, "The Religious Right: Its Agenda, Influence, and Relations with the New Right," *CALC Report,* December 1986, pp. 4-7.

Ultraconservative Christians have a right to participate in the political process and are indeed welcome to be active in it. They have a lot to learn about give and take in a democracy, however, and until they do, they will menace it with demons, angels, and uncompromising certitude.

Since the subject of the Religious Right is so vast and complex, it will be necessary to limit this to a few main points: key issues of the Religious Right and the influence of this militantly active conservative religious movement.. . .

The Religious Right's Agenda

People stirred by Jerry Falwell or James Robison and drawn into active politics for the first time are people who have often been thought of as "outsiders." With the help of television, computers, and savvy politicians, they are beginning to feel "in" at last. They have received a lot of help in the mechanics of politics—such as organizing—but they lack the political give and take that is essential for democracy. While many of the Religious Right's issues and positions are well known, it will be helpful to name and order them.

Family morality issues are extremely important since they reach into the homes of the Religious Right. After all, the impetus for the Religious Right's political activism began with antagonism to the Internal Revenue Service which wanted to deny tax exempt status to Christian schools believed to be in violation of integration legislation.

• The screening of textbooks for evidence of secular humanism is the approach used by those who have children attending public school. Themes such as evolution, cultural relativism in studies of other world cultures, sex education, and values education are of particular concern. Strong attempts are also being made to reinstate prayer in public schools.

• Strengthening the role of the family and the school in discipline can be found in several places in the Family Protection Act.

• Abortion is of course a key family morality issue, so well known as to need no further elaboration.

• Concern about homosexuality ranks high with some Religious Right groups, as does the issue of controlling pornography.

• An anti-ERA stance is also consistent.

• Out of these concerns, book censorship is growing in many communities. This activity of course has a troubling effect upon public and school libraries.

• Monitoring and boycotting the media is another strategy which has developed from these family morality issues and is causing much anxiety in television network circles.

27

JUDEO-CHRISTIAN NATION?

While proponents of the Religious Right have moderated their language of late, describing America as a "Judeo-Christian nation" rather than merely a "Christian nation," their goals have not changed. To them a Judeo-Christian nation means a country where political candidates are judged on the basis of Christian standards of piety and belief, where the public schools are vehicles for the propagation of fundamentalist Christianity, where women are second-class citizens, where gains in civil rights and humanitarian social policies are considered evil, where military spending is limitless, and where support for brutal, right-wing dictators is justified as necessary to keep the world safe from communism.

Anthony T. Podesta, Reform Judaism, *Summer 1986*

Military strength is another important issue for the Religious Right. America may need to "shape up" morally but it should still be "number one" in the world. Only America is to be entrusted with superior power over the rest of the world. In some ways, given the tensions existing in the world today and our nuclear war jitters, this is the most dangerous attitude of the Religious Right. A fear of communism begins to justify any action.

Inflation and the economy cause much anxiety but there is little sense of a program or a platform from the Religious Right on these issues. The Religious Right go along with the New Right on these issues because they are allies. Issues of deregulation, taxes, and the balanced budget do not seem to be the organizing issues of the Religious Right. This is an area in which the Religious Right is easily manipulated.

International issues such as supporting the regime in South Africa and the *contras* in Nicaragua piggyback on family concerns and military power.

The Influence of the Religious Right

In some respects, this is the most difficult question to answer. By underrating the Religious Right, we allow their activity to expand unchecked and unmonitored. By overrating them, however, we become paranoid which serves to expand their influence by our own magnification of it. The following perspectives may be useful in helping us gauge the influence of the Religious Right better.

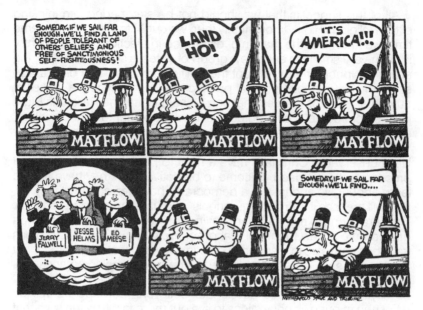

Cartoon by Steve Sack. Reprinted by permission of *Star Tribune, Newspaper of the Twin Cities.*

Despite a media blitz, when a 1980 Gallup Poll asked what the public knew about Moral Majority, 60 percent didn't know of it, 26 percent knew what it was in fact and of these, only 8 percent approved of it and 13 percent disapproved, while the rest didn't know. The media people have found the Religious Right an intriguing and sensational news item, giving it more publicity than it deserves. When a reporter found out that the National Council of Churches of Christ in the U.S.A. (NCC) is a coalition of over 40 million Christians in 32 denominations, she was astounded. "But Moral Majority is probably less than half a million—that's peanuts!" she said.

Evangelicals number at least 30 million, according to Gallup's restrictive definition, and some estimates go as high as 85 million. But these are not to be equated with the Religious Right whose fundamentalism, political conservatism, and political activism are not shared by large numbers of evangelicals. This is a common mistake made by the mass media. The *claims* of various Religious Right groups that they are reaching large numbers of people do not necessarily mean that they are facts. When James Robison sent out a fund-raising letter saying that his television show reached "over 10 million" homes, his claim must be compared with the major rating service's contention that his average weekly audience is less than half a million. The same goes for Pat Robertson and Jerry Falwell.

All of this suggests that we should not be stampeded into thinking of the Religious Right "more highly then we ought to think." At the same time, we know that the margin of difference in elections in this country is often very small, so each new group of votes is significant. Also, the ability to siphon energy, disrupt the political process, and discourage sane and courageous political participation is not simply a matter of numbers. Perhaps the best that can be said is that the Religious Right jars us from complacency, forces us to take another look at ourselves, our own self-righteousness, and to reaffirm our own political involvement.

Let me summarize my own perspective on the Religious Right. Ultraconservative Christians have a right to participate in the political process and are indeed welcome to be active in it. They have a lot to learn about give and take in a democracy, however, and until they do, they will menace it with demons, angels, and uncompromising certitude. They are prone to manipulation, having their own very narrow agenda grafted onto a New Right political program. Our own various religious traditions cause us to respond in differing ways to their involvement but they nudge each of us to reexamine our own postures and maneuvers, even our own handling of Scriptures. If we receive whatever God may be saying through these passionate believers, perhaps we will be refreshed in our own convictions to live out more faithfully the truth that is in *us.*

DEFINING
THE RELIGIOUS RIGHT

A CONSERVATIVE DREAM
FOR AMERICA

Tim LaHaye

The Reverend Tim LaHaye wrote The Race For the 21st Century *in his capacity as the president of the American Coalition for Traditional Values, a network made up of ministers and many of the best-known media evangelists in the nation. His "Capitol Report," which deals with issues that face the family, is televised nationwide via satellite. In* The Race For the 21st Century, *LaHaye tells how the informed Christian can help change America.*

Points to Consider:

1. According to LaHaye, why should you not fear conservative political influence?
2. Who does LaHaye suggest we observe if we want to learn about conservative dreams for America? Why?
3. Explain LaHaye's freedom-with-responsibility philosophy.
4. Why does LaHaye believe it is important for the U.S. to experience a moral-spiritual revival?

Tim LaHaye, *The Race For the 21st Century* (Nashville, Tennessee: Thomas Nelson Publishers, 1986), pp. 119-134. Reprinted with permission of Thomas Nelson Publishers.

It is my prayer, and the prayer of every Christian leader I know, that God will once again visit America with a Great Awakening type revival—just before we race into the 21st century.

No one need fear conservative political influence. Why? First, this is a nation of law, and conservatives are committed to the preservation of the U.S. Constitution. Liberals are the ones who want to rewrite the Constitution or interpret its meaning differently from our Founding Fathers.

Second, the conservative movement is forced to battle the hostile press in seeking to gain the approval and votes of the people. Any violation of their conservative principles would appear on page one and be hammered out on the evening news. Our liberal media would make sure that an inconsistent conservative leadership would be short-lived.

Third, the conservative movement is made up of many diverse groups with differing loyalties and special interests, working voluntarily in union. The margin of victory at the polls is so slim that one group cannot afford to alienate any other faction. I have already noted that this coalition is made up of moderates, old right, New Right, Religious Right, secular conservatives, Catholics, Jews, Protestants, fundamentalists, and others. If one segment begins to dominate the conservative coalition and depart from the conservative political philosophy, the coalition will unravel and come to naught in future elections.

Conservative Dreams for America

If you want a short course in conservative dreams for America, just pay attention to the agenda of Ronald Reagan. Few want more for this country than he does—or have sacrificed more to get it. He could have retired to a well-deserved rest on his beloved ranch at seventy-four years of age. Instead, he plunged into another four years as president to finish what he had begun. Few Americans are afraid of Ronald Reagan's agenda.

In describing the conservative dreams for America, we must keep in mind that although there is basic agreement on the issues, we may find disagreement with regard to priorities. For example, secular conservatives may put a strong national defense first, while we fundamentalist ministers may elevate religious freedom or the protection of human life.

The following list is not intended to represent the conservative movement, for as far as I know, a summit conference has never hammered out such an agenda. This list, which reflects my own thinking, includes the ten moral concerns of the American Coalition for Traditional Values as well as a few other goals evangelicals see as important. . . .

1. Establish religious freedom for all.

If we truly believe our Lord's words, "And you shall know the truth, and the truth shall make you free" (John 8:32), we have nothing to fear in guaranteeing the equal opportunity for all religions to propagate their faith. What we should fear is a totalitarian secularist state that would expel religion from the media (particularly television and radio) as it has from education. While it is true that people are coming to Christ in Russia and China, converts would be multiplied many times if the Christian preachers there had equal access to the media, education, and other means of communication. . . .

2. Pass a human life amendment to reverse *Roe vs. Wade* and render illegal the immoral practice of abortion.

This would not only save millions of unborn babies but would also elevate respect for human life, protect the lives of unwanted or impaired infants (from infanticide), and safeguard the elderly (against euthanasia). We cannot give some government bureaucrats the power to decide who should not continue to live. . . .

If you think a human life amendment is an extreme suggestion, watch the "Living Will" legislation under consideration by the state legislature in Hawaii, the most liberal state in the nation. When first proposed, this legislation offered doctors the right to determine when terminally ill patients could die—without consulting the family. If the humanists try something so bizarre during a conservative revival, can you imagine what they will do if they climb back into the cockpit? . . .

3. Eliminate pornography from both print and video.

If conservative courts cannot find a way to declare porn illegal without violating the First Amendment, then the principle of "liberty with responsibility" may prove adequate. For example, a rape victim ought to be able to sue not only her assailant but also the store that sold the magazine, the distributor, and the publisher if a link to the particular

33

TIM LAHAYE

The Race For The 21ST Century

What Christians must do to survive

Dr. Tim LaHaye, president of the American Coalition for Traditional Values, has been keeping a close watch on the pulse of the nation's affairs and its effects on the church and family. In *The Race For the 21st Century,* he reports those findings and tells how the aware Christian can keep ahead of the changes.

34

magazine can be established. A few such suits could close down the pornography business in a few months. Pornography is only profitable today because publishers do not have to pay for the consequences of the moral holocaust they unleash.

4. Establish a strong national defense.

Government's primary purpose is to protect its citizens from attack, both foreign and domestic. In a world threatened by communism's well-advertised intentions of world conquest, it is the supreme duty of government to arm sufficiently so as to defend citizens against the plight of 40 percent of the rest of the world's population, which today is enslaved by communism. Some conservatives put this at the top of the agenda. I would have no quarrel with that, for if we lose our freedoms to a Communist dictator, we will forfeit our Constitution and all other rights. . . .

5. Adopt a freedom-with-responsibility philosophy.

If our courts adopt a freedom-with-responsibility philosophy, crime would be extremely unprofitable. Suppose an armed robber shoots a father of three children and is sent to prison. Under this philosophy, the judge and jury would require him to work within a penal system to pay for the support of those children and their mother. After all, the robber killed their means of support; he should be required to replace it. In like manner, the man who rapes a woman and causes her pregnancy should pay for the cost of his crime to both woman and child. Conservatives are not opposed to freedom, but we do favor that it be reasonably balanced with responsibility.

6. Halt deficit spending and eliminate government waste, unnecessary bureaucracy, and uncontrolled spending.

"Buy now and pay later" is contrary to biblical principles. With a national debt in excess of $2 trillion, we must begin to pay for our past. If we do not, we assure poverty for our children. . . .

Almost everyone agrees that government is horrendously wasteful. The well-publicized Peter Grace Report has been largely ignored by government workers, but it still contains 2,478 separate, distinct, and specific. . .cost cutting, revenue-enhancing recommendations for government. . . .The Grace Report favors cost-cutting changes over increasing personal income tax. I believe that most American citizens would agree. A conservative government should resist the temptation of all governments to increase its size, costs, and control over people. We need reduction, not expansion. . . .

7. Change our inept welfare system to an effective people rehabilitation program.

Since welfare office centers are usually urban, welfare has contributed to ghettoizing our major cities, where the poor are drawn away from the best job markets to terrible living conditions and a perpetuated dependency on government support. Third-generation welfare recipients are now common. The aid to dependent families, a welcome support for widows and abandoned women with small children, is now a means of livelihood as girls purposely get themselves pregnant for the fourth and fifth time. An inner-city school teacher told me recently that during a discussion of intended vocations one girl told her, "I don't need any more education. I'm planning to get pregnant four or five times, and the government will support me—just like my mother."

An inner-city pastor reported to a group of ministers that welfare was actually encouraging couples to get divorced since two people living separately receive higher monthly payments than do husband and wife. The same is true for some senior citizens who would like to marry but live together out of wedlock because if they marry, retirement checks go down.

Somehow we need to abandon the idea that government owes people a living. Government should not be responsible for people except in emergencies, the threat of violence (foreign or domestic), calamities, or disaster. No American would object to welfare helping disaster victims or widows with children. But unending aid to the able-bodied who refuse to work because they can make more money staying at home is not only a national disgrace and a defrauding of the taxpayers but a crime against the poor, who need to be encouraged to get out and work. While it may be true that learning skills on the job often provides take-home pay no larger than welfare payments, the individual's self-respect takes a giant step forward. . . .

The government would greatly serve its citizens by launching a national advertising campaign to acquaint citizens with adult educational opportunities (much as they use television to recruit service personnel for the military). A few thousand dollars to upgrade the skills of its workers is a proper government investment, for such monies will be returned many times in increased taxes. Unfortunately, welfare payments are often little more than wasted money that creates tragic human dependency. . . .

8. Get the federal government out of education and make the educational process competitive by allowing tuition tax credits or vouchers for parents to use at the schools of their choice.

In my book *The Battle for the Public Schools,* I demonstrate that tax vouchers would improve education by making it compete for the approval of its customers—parents! Educators deplore the idea, trying desperately to convince parents that it would ruin education. By contrast it would have the same effect on education that foreign imports have had on the auto industry. In the early seventies, when auto makers were unresponsive to the design desires of the people, Japan met those desires and forced Detroit to follow suit. . . .

If educators had to compete for students within a broad spectrum of private, parochial, and public schools, you can be sure they would please the parents by offering a quality education—or get out of the business. Any government that spends over $260 million dollars a year on education is in the education business. . . .

9. Develop greater participation in the political process by Christians and other religiously committed citizens.

If born-again Christians represent "4 out of 10 people" in the population, we ought to aim for 40 percent of the seats in Congress, the cabinet, and other areas of influence in government, media, and education. I am not calling for government quotas, as liberal critics often accuse. We simply need to establish goals on the part of the Christian community and all other citizens who share our religious values. . . .This same goal should be held by Catholic, Jewish, and other religious citizens also. We would serve future generations well if all religious citizens of the nation became more involved in the political process, not only as candidates but as voters and campaign volunteers. . . .

Politicians whose voting records or published positions conflict with traditional values should have no place in a government based on the Judeo-Christian heritage of America. Certainly they are welcome to live here in freedom and enjoy every protection of the law, but the religious people whose taxes provide their salaries and whose votes determine their positions in office have both a right and a duty to elect representation in keeping with their values—regardless of political party.

10. Establish a television network committed to truth and traditional values.

We do not have free media in America but a liberally controlled press and entertainment industry. Although it is less than forty years old, television is becoming increasingly awesome in its influence on the thinking of this nation. I find it ironic that all four networks—ABC, CBS, NBC, and the so-called Public Broadcasting System (PBS)—are overwhelmingly liberal.

We need at least one conservative network to offer an alternative to the liberal bias we are usually confronted with on network newscasts. . . .

11. Use American technology and agriculture to help the suffering and impoverished throughout the world.

It seems obscene to pay American farmers $21 billion a year *not* to farm while starving people throughout the world are crying for our help.

There must be some way to use this money in the purchase of wheat, corn, and other staples so Third World nations friendly to our government could sustain life.

If the only reason the American farmer is not free to feed the world is that this action would destroy the world's economy, we need to re-evaluate our national priorities. A people-to-people food program would go a long way toward bettering relations between us and less fortunate nations, and it would save countless numbers of lives. Admittedly there are complications to such a program, but until we adopt an all-encompassing project, the plight of hungry nations will not be remedied. . . .

12. Ensure the world's safety from nuclear attack.

Trillions of dollars have been spent by the Communist and non-Communist countries in producing the most frightening military buildup in world history. Today both sides have enough nuclear arms to destroy the world *several* times over. It is now time for the United States to use its technological superiority to protect the world from a universal holocaust. Such a plan, admittedly in its developmental status, is the president's Strategic Defense Initiative (SDI) or Star Wars program. This defense umbrella, or one like it, will have the capacity to destroy in-coming missiles out in space long before they can reach their targets and thus render nuclear arms obsolete.

If such a possibility exists, we owe it to the world to develop and use it—not only for our own national protection, but for that of all countries. Through American ingenuity we can implement a program that will make the 21st century free of the constant fear of nuclear destruction. America should be morally strong enough to embark on such a worthy goal. . . .

13. Reaffirm America as a religious country rather than a secular nation.

Conservatives do not want a Protestant or Catholic government that uses its power to coerce unbelievers or confuse doctrine with law. Government, however, should not be hostile to religion—as it is rapidly becoming today. Unless this trend is reversed, the small number of secularizers (a term I use to denote those whose goal is to secularize our society) in influential positions will continue to remove our historic religious recognition. It is a tragic distortion of our Constitution and the intent of our Founding Fathers that Christmas carols must be kept out of public schools and that sexual promiscuity between unwed teens cannot be labeled as immoral (not to mention a health hazard)—all to avoid offending the 6 percent of the nation's atheists. That America is *not* a secular nation needs to be officially reaffirmed. This would not only allow voluntary school prayer but would make it possible for our teachers to introduce character training into their curriculum. . . .

14. A Moral-Spiritual Revival

Most members of the conservative/born-again coalition look for a moral spiritual revival. I am convinced that unless this nation experiences revival similar to the Great Awakening, the United States is doomed to repeat the paths of decadent societies before us. A political revival is not enough. We must have a moral-spiritual revival like those that shook the American society to its very foundations, maintaining an impact on the nation for decades. . . .

It is my prayer, and the prayer of every Christian leader I know, that God will once again visit America with a Great Awakening type revival— just before we race into the 21st century.

DEFINING
THE RELIGIOUS RIGHT

A REACTIONARY VISION
FOR THE FUTURE

Patrick M. Arnold

Patrick M. Arnold, S.J., wrote this article in his capacity as assistant professor of religious studies at St. Louis University, and is presently a visiting professor of Old Testament at the Jesuit School of Theology in Berkeley, California. His article appeared in America, *a weekly, Catholic Jesuit publication on moral and public affairs.*

Points to Consider:

1. Compare and contrast the author's definitions of conservatism and fundamentalism.
2. Explain why fundamentalists frequently use force or violence to achieve their goals.
3. Why are modern-day fundamentalists closely allied with right-wing or repressive political regimes?
4. Describe the five characteristics of fundamentalism.

Most broadly speaking, fundamentalism is a historically recurring tendency within the Judeo-Christian-Muslim religious traditions that regularly erupts in reaction to cultural change.

It is extremely important at the outset of this reading to distinguish between conservatism and fundamentalism. Conservatism may be described broadly as a philosophy that values established, traditional ideas and practices, and seeks to preserve a given community's historical heritage—especially in times of cultural change....

What, then, is fundamentalism? In its narrowest American definition, fundamentalism is popularly understood as a native Protestant movement that began after 1910 in reaction to liberal biblical interpretation. Fundamentalism is actually a modern version of Christianity that stresses biblical literalism, premillennialism, and absolute moral rules....

Most broadly speaking, fundamentalism is a historically recurring tendency within the Judeo-Christian-Muslim religious traditions that regularly erupts in reaction to cultural change. Psychological studies describe its strongest adherents as "authoritarian personalities": individuals who feel threatened in a world of conspiring evil forces, who think in simplistic and stereotypical terms and who are attracted to authoritarian and moralistic answers to their problems.

When cultural stresses reach critical proportions, these individuals evidently tend to spur powerful movements within their respective religious traditions....The global fundamentalism of the 1980s thus represents an unhealthy attempt to prevent religion's feared demise through the use of force and even violence....

The explosive capabilities of fundamentalism first became evident within Islam. Iran experienced the horrors of Shiite violence in the late 1970s during the revolution that brought the Ayatollah Khomeini to power. Later, tensions erupted within Sunni communities in Syria and Egypt as a result of activities of the *ikwan islami* or "Muslim brotherhood," who were instrumental in the assassination of President Anwar el-Sadat in 1981.

Shortly thereafter, "ultraorthodox" (*haredim*) movements developed in Israel. These groups split from the traditional "orthodox" (*hasidim*) community, which had coexisted somewhat uneasily with the rest of Israeli society. They split on the grounds that the *hasidim* had become too tolerant, and the *haridim* violently began to demand theocratic changes in Israeli law and society. Riots broke out in the streets of Jerusalem in 1986, and angry Jews even began to deface the synagogues of their opponents.

Modern fundamentalism first burst upon the American scene vividly during the 1980 Presidential election with the rise of right-wing religious and political coalitions of unprecedented strength. While less virulent than the Middle Eastern strains of the disease, American fundamentalism occasionally breaks out in episodes such as the violent bombings of abortion clinics, anti-Semitic incidents, attacks on blacks by white "Christian" sects, and even in attempts in local schools and libraries to ban textbooks or novels that smack of "secular humanism."

The Catholic community was not to prove entirely immune from this disease. In the last few years, indications have grown that the fundamentalist virus is mutating and beginning to produce Catholic symptoms. That this neo-orthodox movement is an illness, and not a genuine reform, is first of all suggested by its affinities with the contemporary problems afflicting Islam, Judaism, and Protestantism. At least five unhealthy characteristics are visible within the movements threatening all these religions.

1. Fundamentalism is a reactionary emotional movement that develops within cultures experiencing social crisis. Uncritical and insensitive radical-liberal changes in the 1960s and 1970s, in conjunction with dizzying technological advances, appear to have provided the immediate stimulus to the reactionary worldwide Zeitgeist* of the 1980s. Fundamentalism at root feeds on fear and anger and, in many ways, provides opportunities for revenge upon agents of change.

In the Middle East, both the Shiites and the Muslim brotherhood project these emotions on all agents of Westernization, especially the "Great Satan" (the United States) and its allies. In Israel, the Jewish *haredim* react violently to technological and social changes accompanying 20th-century secularization in the belief that the religious truths of Judaism are endangered.

---

*Editor's note: According to the *American Heritage Dictionary of the English Language,* Zeitgeist is a German word that means "the spirit of the time; the taste and outlook characteristic of a period or generation."

42

Cartoon by William Sanders. Reprinted with special permission of NAS, Inc.

In the United States, the phrase "secular humanism" encapsulates all that is threatening to reactionary Protestants and Catholics alike. For Christian fundamentalists, the term implies a conscious conspiracy of liberals, media, and government to undermine America's religious heritage.

Recently, for example, leading Catholic reactionaries (claiming to be "ecumenical") joined Protestant fundamentalists in testifying on behalf of plaintiffs attempting to ban from the Alabama school system books that allegedly promoted the "religion of secular humanism." The near-paranoia of this attitude is revealed by continual studies that show that American religious commitment and activity, always strong, is increasing in modern times. . . .

2. Perhaps the most revealing and dangerous characteristic of fundamentalists is that their fear and rage are directed, not primarily at the actual agents of secularization (atheists, agnostics, or enemies of religion), but mainly at coreligionists who appear to have adapted all too well to modernity through unholy compromise. The failure of liberals or moderates to employ violence or force against "the enemy" is proof of their laxity, if not conspiracy. The fact that coreligionists may equally well be concerned with dangers to religion and morals, and yet choose different methods of addressing these problems, is frequently disregarded.

Fundamentalism is therefore always religiously divisive and is marked by attempts to purge, persecute, or oppress liberals, moderates, and even conservatives who have "lost the true faith." In its most extreme form, this purge is accomplished through execution or massacre. *Assassin,* the Arabic word for fundamentalist, implies one method of eliminating leading members of the religious opposition. Killing and torture have marked the fundamentalist outbreak of the 1980s in the Middle East.

In the United States, fundamentalists seem content with driving the opposition out of the religious community through formal excommunication, firing, or silencing. In the last decade, a number of rightward-drifting Protestant churches have expelled ministers and theologians who refused to abandon liberal or moderate principles. The Lutheran Missouri Synod, for example, forced out an entire theological faculty (Seminex) that would not accede to the new fundamentalist agenda including biblical literalism; a similar development is already well underway in elements of the Southern Baptist Convention. . . .

Theologians and religious women, however, have proved the most vulnerable to the purge. Since fundamentalists regard diversity as chaos, variant theological ideas, moral approaches, and even altered religious garb are said to sow "confusion" in the ranks of the faithful. Theological or moral opinions different from those of fundamentalists are "dissent," and dissent is "disloyalty." Once disloyal sisters or theologians have been identified, they are then subject to powerful internal pressures, letter-writing campaigns, silencing, intimidation, or even expulsion in the name of "peace" in the church. . . .

3. A universal feature of fundamentalists is their captivity by what might be called the "myth of the Golden Age." Fleeing from the exaggerated evils of contemporary society, they seek the glorious days of their religious founders, an imaginary past edited of its own actual terrors.

The attempt of Shiite revolutionaries to restore Iran to a medieval theocratic state, or of ultraorthodox Israelis to create a theocracy along biblical lines, are well known. In the United States, Protestant evangelicals pine for "that old time religion" of the 19th century. . . .

4. Fundamentalists insist upon the absolute, infallible, inerrant, and unambiguous authority of official religious texts. While Muslims proclaim the authority of the Arabic Koran as God's direct word, orthodox Jews consider each word of the Hebrew Torah to be directly inspired. One frequently gets the impression that some Protestant sects believe in the absolute inerrancy of the Bible as given in the original English.

The difference between Catholic reactionaries and Protestant evangelicals regarding Scripture has made it difficult to recognize Catholic fundamentalism. Neo-orthodox Catholics rarely even mention the Bible, except insofar as it provides proof-texts for ecclesial authority or favorite moral concerns. In place of Scripture, however, stand the official written statements of the Roman magisterium, the highest Catholic teaching office. Not only is defined dogma infallible, but every teaching that proceeds from the Vatican is to be obeyed absolutely.

In practice, of course, the fundamentalist Catholic selection process amid these infallible teachings is a highly arbitrary one, as it is in all other sects. In the main, church teachings regarding questions of authority or private sexual morality are given enormous weight. Any attempts to nuance or contextualize these directives bring accusations of heterodoxy. Yet church teachings regarding social questions such as poverty, nuclear warfare, labor and human rights are, at best, regarded as matter for debate and at worst, dismissed as "interference with politics.". . .

5. Fundamentalists in the 1980s are usually closely allied with right-wing or repressive political regimes in the hope of advancing theocratic policies. The totalitarian religious dictatorship of Khomeini's Iran, of course, is well known. Israel's orthodox groups, meanwhile, compose a formidable coalition with the rightist Likud party, hoping to win greater religious control over secular Israeli society in exchange for support for Likud's militaristic agenda.

In the United States, the partisan political pretensions of many Protestant evangelical leaders are increasingly apparent. Groups such as the Rev. Jerry Falwell's Moral Majority have become little more than staging areas for Republican political campaigns and conservative lobbying. Evangelist Pat Robertson is in the process of converting his television audience into a political base as he campaigns for the Republican Presidential nomination.

Catholic fundamentalists have proceeded more cautiously and subtly into right-wing politicization. Ronald Reagan effectively co-opted Catholic antiabortionists by running as a pro-life candidate in 1980. Despite his failure to deliver the slightest return for this support during (or since) his first term, President Reagan increased his hold on Catholic conservatives in 1984. According to NBC News reports during that election, leading Catholic hierarchical officials were enlisted in a campaign to discredit Democratic Vice-Presidential candidate Geraldine Ferraro by focusing Catholic attention solely on the abortion issue. The attempts of Cardinal Joseph L. Bernardin of Chicago to sketch out a consistent pro-life "seamless garment" ethic won him the instant vilification of the fundamentalists, who successfully suggested to millions of Catholics that they must consider a candidate's "abortion record" before any other issue. . . .

What is, perhaps, most revealing about fundamentalism, and in the end what gives it away as a religious disease, is *what it fails to discuss, promote, or preach*. Neo-orthodox tracts are replete with references to doctrine, truth, morality, orthodoxy, salvation, error, and dissent. Yet they rarely mention Jesus Christ or the kind of moral issues that evidently most concerned Him: greed, religious hypocrisy, or misuse of authority. For all their outcry against secularism, their writings are largely bereft of any spirituality, preferring instead either partisan political topics or subjects of a largely intramural, ecclesiastical nature.

DEFINING
THE RELIGIOUS RIGHT

CAUSA INTERNATIONAL:
THE POINT

CAUSA International

The Reverend Sun Myung Moon, founder of the International Unification Church, created CAUSA International in Washington, D.C. in 1980. CAUSA International is the political arm of the Unification Church, designed to provide Latin Americans with an ideological framework in their struggle against communism. CAUSA has now expanded beyond Latin America and become global in scope, being active in the U.S., Europe, and Africa.

Points to Consider:

1. Compare and contrast CAUSA International's definitions of Godism and communism.
2. Describe the five main points of the CAUSA Worldview.
3. Analyze the parallels between the CAUSA Worldview and the beliefs of the American Founding Fathers.
4. How does CAUSA International plan to achieve the Free World's survival?

CAUSA International, *Introduction to the CAUSA Worldview* (New York: CAUSA Institute, 1985), pp. 383-390. Reprinted with permission of CAUSA International.

In CAUSA there is hope. For the first time, we see hope of reversing the tide in our deadly struggle between freedom and communist tyranny. For the first time we see real hope for America and for the world. CAUSA brings a new day of hope.

The following is a brief summary of the CAUSA Worldview:

Godism vs. Communism: Two Worldviews

Godism advocates a change in man, while communism advocates a change in the economic system. Godism advocates an internal revolution within the human being, the change from selfishness to unselfishness. Communism advocates an external and violent revolution in line with its ideological perspective.

Godism aspires to deal directly with the fundamental moral corruption which pervades all systems. Communism deals only with the symptoms of these problems.

The Importance of the Individual

The key is the individual. On the individual level the deviation of man from God began. Likewise it is on this level where restoration must also begin. If individuals are changed, then naturally families will be changed. Then the communities, nations, and the entire world which these families live in will be transformed.

God or no God?

Godism maintains that there is a God; communism postulates that there is not. Godism maintains that life is eternal; communism states that man is a temporal being. Godism believes that there are absolute values; communism is based upon relative values. Godism espouses cooperation in human relations centered upon love; communism emphasizes the dialectic centered upon hatred. Godism recognizes that there are many struggles in human life, but in essence, these are between good and evil, selfishness and unselfishness. Communism identifies the basic form of struggle as class struggle.

Ultimately it can all be reduced to a single belief. Godism maintains that there is a God; communism denies this. Only one of these beliefs can be true. We find the answer in the living reality of God.

Five Points of the CAUSA Worldview

The following five points are the succinct expression of the CAUSA Worldview. We feel that these five points are broad enough to encompass the beliefs of all God-accepting people as well as people of con-

48

science. At the same time, these five points are specific enough to exclude all communistic and atheist ideas.

If you can accept these five principles, or even one of them, we would like you to work with CAUSA. These are the five points CAUSA feels all religious people and people of conscience can accept and unite upon. We are confident that a communist is not able to accept even one of the following principles, which represent the foundation of CAUSA.

The CAUSA Worldview maintains that:

1. God is the Creator.
2. Man is the child of God.
3. Man is created free to love and take responsibility.
4. Man lives an eternal life.
5. Selfless love is the supreme value.

Parallels Between the CAUSA Worldview and Beliefs of the American Founding Fathers

These five points run closely parallel with the principles affirmed several hundred years ago by the Founding Fathers of America. Dr. Cleon Skousen, founder of the National Center of Constitutional Studies and a leading expert on the U.S. Constitution, in his text *The Five Thousand Year Leap,* explains that the United States of America accomplished in little more than a hundred years what required thousands of years to bring about in other parts of the world. The reason, according to Dr. Skousen, is that the Founding Fathers placed a high priority on religion and moral values.

This priority is very evident when we consider that the same Congress which approved the United States Constitution also passed the Northwest Ordinance of 1787. Article 3 of this ordinance states: "Religion, morality, and knowledge being necessary to good government and the happiness of mankind, schools and the means of education shall forever be encouraged."

Illustration of Reverend Sun Myung Moon by Ron Swanson

The Founding Fathers believed that education should include not only the teaching of knowledge, but religion and morality as well. Today, however, the U.S. public school system devotes little effort to the education of moral values. Religious teaching in the schools has often been replaced with secular humanist principles which are, in essence, atheistic. While many oppose the re-inclusion of religious principles in the American public school curriculum because they do not want their children to be indoctrinated in the beliefs of a particular denomination, the fact is that the Founding Fathers set out from the beginning to make the teaching of religion a unifying cultural factor in education and to exclude any emphasis on a particular creed or doctrine. They sought a universal religious code that would be acceptable to people of all faiths.

Benjamin Franklin offered one expression of this universal code when he expressed the following articles of faith:

> Here is my creed: I believe in One God, the Creator of the universe. That He governs it by His Providence. That He ought to be worshipped. That the most acceptable service we render to Him is in doing good to His other children. That the soul of man is immortal and will be treated with justice in another life respecting its conduct in this. These I take to be the fundamental points in all sound religion.

When we summarize it we arrive at the following five points:

1. One God, the creator of the universe, is to be worshipped.
2. He governs the world by His Providence.
3. Men can glorify God by loving His children.
4. The soul of man is immortal.
5. In the next life, the soul of man is judged by his conduct in this world.

This formulation, or something closely resembling it, seems to have commanded the widespread respect of the Founding Fathers. Samuel Adams, commenting on these points, said, "This group of basic beliefs which constitute the religion of America is the religion of all mankind."

CAUSA believes that the fact that the American Founding Fathers were thinking not only of America, but of all mankind, is quite significant. God's will is ultimately to unite all mankind into one world family of God.

We would like to express the contrast and similarity between the Founding Fathers' "universal religious code" and the CAUSA Worldview in a little more detail. The Founding Fathers expressed the belief that God is the Creator and is to be worshipped. It is not CAUSA's intention to promote any particular form of worship or doctrine of salvation. That is the mission of the various churches. Therefore we say "God is the Creator."

To the Founding Fathers' article of faith, "He governs the world by His Providence," CAUSA adds that "man is created free so that he can love and take responsibility," thus emphasizing that man must take part in God's providence by exerting his free will. "The soul of man is immortal" and "Man lives an eternal life," are, of course, identical in content. Finally, the Founding Fathers believed that "the soul of man is

51

judged by his conduct in this world." The fifth point of the CAUSA Worldview, which states that "selfless love is the supreme value," underlines the standard for the judgement of man's earthly life and the main criterion for the growth of the human spirit. When man has successfully practiced a life of selfless love here on earth, his spirit will be free to commune with God and enjoy fellowship with all people in the eternal hereafter.

CAUSA Pursues Traditional Values

The parallel between the CAUSA Worldview and the above-mentioned points of faith of the Founding Fathers is not coincidental. Just as the Founding Fathers of America believed that religious life was going to be vital for the survival of America, so CAUSA sees it as being crucial for the survival of the Free World. And as the hope of the Free World today lies with America, CAUSA urges America to return to its founding spirit. It is the fervent hope of CAUSA that these presentations will engender a new strength of religious zeal, and that each CAUSA participant, whatever his or her religion may be, will be inspired to a new energy of dedication to God and mankind.

In CAUSA there is hope. For the first time, we see hope of reversing the tide in our deadly struggle between freedom and communist tyranny. For the first time we see real hope for America and for the world. CAUSA brings a new day of hope.

8

DEFINING
THE RELIGIOUS RIGHT

CAUSA INTERNATIONAL: THE COUNTERPOINT

Fred Clarkson and Sara Diamond

The following comments by Fred Clarkson and Sara Diamond were reprinted from Sequoia, *a national, liberal newsmonthly for concerned churchpeople.*

Fred Clarkson wrote this article in his capacity as contributing editor of Interchange Report, *a quarterly journal that monitors trends in conservative politics. Sara Diamond is a Berkeley-based, freelance writer for both print media, radio, and television.*

Points to Consider:

1. Would democracy survive in CAUSA's unified world? Why or why not?
2. Explain why the Unification Church has shifted its focus from street sales to inter-denominational outreach.
3. Why do followers of the Reverend Sun Myung Moon believe he is the Messiah?
4. What does Sara Diamond mean when she says that "the actions of the Unification Church speak louder than words"?

Fred Clarkson and Sara Diamond, "Meet Rev. Moon: 'The Messiah': Learn of his Organizations and Actions to Take Over the World," *Sequoia,* March-April 1986, p. 9.

by Fred Clarkson

Sun Myung Moon is the new Messiah, according to Moonist doctrine not proclaimed in public. The Korean-born evangelist is to bend America to "God's will," leading to a final war over Soviet communism that will bring about the Kingdom of Heaven on Earth.

Moon is best known as a controversial leader of a religious cult that allegedly uses deception and brain-washing to gain and keep recruits. When parents and friends conspire with 'deprogrammers' to snap their loved ones out of it, a different controversy arises.

Much less well known are the political activities and extremism of the Unification church and its satellite organizations.

CAUSA: Moon's Political Arm

Moon asserted in a 1973 speech that he will impose an "automatic theocracy to rule the world." The principal vehicle Moon is using in this quest is CAUSA, his political organization. CAUSA, originally an acronym for Confederation of the Associations for the Unification of the Societies of the Americas, now promotes a theocratic ideology called "Unificationism" or "Godism," a comprehensive world view that can unify the world's religions against communism.

Democracy would not likely survive in this atmosphere. "The more democratic a society is," Moon asserted in a speech reprinted in CAUSA magazine last year, "the more serious the collapse of its traditional value system appears to be. This shows that democracy has failed to provide solutions to problems facing our society and the world."

CAUSA, founded in 1980, has distinguished itself through its collaboration with some of the most repugnant military dictatorships in the world, including Chile, Paraguay, and the former military regimes of Bolivia and Argentina.

A CAUSAesque glimpse of Moon's Kingdom of Heaven on Earth may have been provided by CAUSA head Bo Hi Pak, who has said of the notorious Paraguayan dictator Gen. Alfredo Stroessner: "I believe he's a special man, chosen by God to run his country."

Anti-Semitic References

Anti-Semitism is a chilling aspect of the Moonist world view. The *Divine Principle,* the main theological work of Unificationism, contains 125 anti-Semitic references, according to the American Jewish Committee. Moon himself has said: "By killing one man, Jesus, the Jewish people had to suffer 2,000 years. During the Second World War six million people were slaughtered to cleanse all the sins of the Jewish people for the killing of Jesus."

54

by Sara Diamond

In its quest to defeat communism, Rev. Sun Myung Moon's Unification Church has had a history of involvement with conservative and far-right organizations in the United States and abroad. Moon received a special "guest of honor" seat at President Reagan's 1981 inauguration and, since its inception in 1980, Moon's political arm CAUSA has collaborated with military regimes in Honduras, Bolivia, Paraguay, and Uruguay, not to mention CAUSA's role as a major "private donor" to the Nicaraguan contra rebels.

In 1984 Rev. Moon went to prison for a variety of crimes—filing false tax returns, obstructing justice, perjury, and submitting false documents to the Justice Department—and since that time, he and his followers have waged a public relations campaign for the support of the religious community.

"Religious Freedom"

The campaign revolves around the murky concept of "religious freedom" and the assertion by Moon and some Christian ministers that the U.S. government is selectively prosecuting church leaders. The issue has spurred unprecedented support for Rev. Moon from both fundamentalist and mainline clergy.

In May 1984 more than 300 clergy gathered in Washington, D.C. for a Religious Freedom rally in support of Rev. Moon. The rally was organized by veteran civil rights leader Rev. Joseph Lowery of the Southern Christian Leadership Conference and Rev. Tim LaHaye, former head of the California Moral Majority. Also prominent at the event were Christian Voice chairman Rev. Bob Grant and New York Civil Liberties Union President Jeremiah Gutman, whose law firm has been on retainer for the Unification Church for many years. The clergy formed the Ad Hoc Committee for Religious Freedom; later, with a $500,000 grant from the Unification Church, the Coalition for Religious Freedom was formed. The original advisory board included some of the leading TV evangelists—Jimmy Swaggart, James Robison, Rex Humbard, Paul

Crouch (Trinity Broadcast Network), author Hal Lindsey, and Dr. Ben Armstrong, Director of the National Religious Broadcasters.

I first stumbled across this Ad Hoc Committee in August 1984 when I saw a Religious Freedom Rally poster on a University of California-Berkeley bulletin board. On August 30, 1984, three hundred people—about half Black Baptists and the rest Moonies—gathered at the Center of Hope Community Church in East Oakland. It was a lively evening of patriotic music and rousing speeches by Rev. Joseph Lowery, Rev. Donald Sills of Glendale, California, and Rev. Moon's daughter In Jin Moon. Three Oakland politicians—Mayor Lionel Wilson, Alameda County Supervisor John George, and Oakland City Councilmember Wilson Riles, Jr. (then a candidate for Oakland Mayor)—were also on hand. Mayor Wilson and Supervisor George made a few unmemorable remarks. But, to my surprise, Wilson Riles, Jr. stood up and announced that "Oakland is a Christian city and we intend it to stay that way."

Improving Their Image

I later learned that Moon's imprisonment in June 1984 was followed by similar "rallies" in churches across the country, and that the Unification Church had shifted its focus from street sales and converting people to inter-denominational outreach. In early 1985 the Moonies spent over $4 million to send packets of books and videocassettes to 300,000 ministers. The materials were designed to explain Unification doctrine and dispel some of the negative stereotypes about Rev. Moon as a cult leader.

The goal of the expensive campaign was summed up best in the internal Unification newsletter quoted by journalist Fred Clarkson in *Christianity and Crisis* (Oct. 28, 1985). Rev. Ken Sudo told Unification leaders in May 1985, "Father went into Danbury [prison] as the leader of the Unification Church, but when he comes out, he must be the leader of the Free World."

Moon: The Messiah

Followers of the Rev. Moon believe that he is the Messiah. Moon's *Divine Principle* teaches that because Christ did not marry and have children, His mission was unfulfilled; therefore Moon was sent to establish the true Kingdom on Earth. Moon and his followers see communism, which they equate with Satanism, as the chief obstacle to the establishment of an "automatic theocracy" where Moon will control all of society's leadership—clergy, media, government, education, and the sciences.

In pursuit of that goal, the Unification Church has made alliances with other New Right groups. In 1984 CAUSA gave the National Conservative Political Action Committee (NICPAC) $500,000 to lobby for Star Wars and for aid to the Nicaraguan *contra*. And a January 1986 *Mother Jones* article revealed a financial link between Rev. Tim LaHaye's

American Coalition for Traditional Values (ACTV) and Moon's top aid and CAUSA International president, Bo Hi Pak.

The Struggle for Political Power

The Unification Church has been directly involved in determining the leadership of at least one government. Germany's *Stern* magazine, in an investigation of former Nazi Klaus Barbie's role in the successful 1980 military coup in Bolivia, found that CAUSA had spent $4 million in the coup plot. Longtime Moonie Thomas Ward (now vice president of CAUSA) worked with Barbie out of the Bolivia CAUSA office and delivered CIA payments to an Argentine agent involved in the coup.

The Moonies understand that the struggle for political power is, above all, an "ideological struggle." That's why the Unification Church has taken thousands of journalists on all-expense-paid tours of Asia, Central America, and the Soviet Union. And that's why, in 1985 alone, CAUSA recruited some 10,000 non-Moonies to attend all-expense-paid conferences on the nature of "communism."

Recruiting Others for "The Cause"

Even after Moon's release from prison last fall, the Coalition for Religious Freedom continues to be the Moonies' major recruiting arm. Local and regional boards of directors are comprised of ministers of various denominations, but CRF conferences are staffed primarily by Unification Church members, and participants are urged to attend CAUSA lectures. Leadership between the two organizations overlaps; for example, Rev. John Lane, pastor of Grace Baptist Church of San Francisco, is vice president of the California Committee for Religious Freedom and also sits on CAUSA's regional board.

Lane is one of, literally, thousands of black ministers recruited into Unification organizations since Moon's conviction. From the Moonies' standpoint, the black church is a fertile recruiting ground; black ministers have a tradition of political activism and cam empathize with Moon's claims of persecution.

That empathy is one-sided, however. According to investigative reporter Murray Waas, various Moon businesses overseas received five $900,000 payments totalling $4.5 million from the South African government, as part of its official foreign media-buying program. In exchange, the Moonie-owned *Washington Times* newspaper has consistently editoralized against divestment and sanctions toward the Botha regime, and has attempted to discredit anti-apartheid leaders in the U.S. and in South Africa.

Whether The Cause is "fighting Communism" or "defending Religious Freedom," it seems that the actions of the Unification Church speak louder than words.

WHAT IS EDITORIAL BIAS?

This activity may be used as an individualized study guide for students in libraries and resource centers or as a discussion catalyst in small group and classroom discussions.

The capacity to recognize an author's point of view is an essential reading skill. The skill to read with insight and understanding involves the ability to detect different kinds of opinions or bias. Sex bias, race bias, ethnocentric bias, political bias, and religious bias are five basic kinds of opinions expressed in editorials and all literature that attempts to persuade. They are briefly defined below.

---

5 Kinds of Editorial Opinion or Bias

SEX BIAS—The expression of dislike for and/or feeling of superiority over a person because of gender or sexual preference

RACE BIAS—The expression of dislike for and/or feeling of superiority over a racial group

ETHNOCENTRIC BIAS—The expression of a belief that one's own group, race, religion, culture, or nation is superior. Ethnocentric persons judge others by their own standards and values.

POLITICAL BIAS—The expression of opinions and attitudes about government-related issues on the local, state, national, or international level

RELIGIOUS BIAS—The expression of a religious belief or attitude

---

Guidelines

1. From the readings in chapter one, locate five sentences that provide examples of editorial opinion or bias.

2. Write down each of the above sentences and determine what kind of bias each sentence represents. Is it *sex bias, race bias, ethnocentric bias, political bias, or religious bias?*

3. Make up one sentence statements that would be an example of each of the following: *sex bias, race bias, ethnocentric bias, political bias, and religious bias.*

4. See if you can locate five sentences that are factual statements from the readings in chapter one.

CHAPTER 2

FOREIGN POLICY
AND THE MILITARY

9

FOREIGN POLICY
AND THE MILITARY

THE THEOLOGY
OF NUCLEAR WAR:
THE POINT

Hal Lindsey

Hal Lindsey is one of the latest of the Armageddon preachers. He is also the author of several books, including The Late Great Planet Earth, *a book that sold more than 18 million copies. According to the* New York Times, The Late Great Planet Earth *was the top nonfiction best-seller of the 1970s. Lindsey attended the University of Houston and graduated from the School of Theology at Dallas Theological Seminary.*

Points to Consider:

1. Summarize the three events that will secure Israel's place in the prophetic puzzle.
2. How does Russia fit into the prophetic puzzle? What evidence does Lindsey provide to support this position?
3. Describe "the Rapture."
4. Analyze the events Lindsey predicted in 1970. Have any of these events occurred?

Hal Lindsey (with C. C. Carlson), *The Late Great Planet Earth* (Grand Rapids, MI: Zondervan Publishing House, 1970). Taken from *The Late Great Planet Earth* by Hal Lindsey and C. C. Carlson. Copyright © 1970 by Zondervan Publishing House. Used by permission.

As we see the world becoming more chaotic, we can be "steadfast" and "immovable," because we know where it's going and where we are going. We know that Christ will protect us until His purpose is finished and then He will take us to be with Himself.

We believe there is hope for the future, in spite of the way the world looks today. We believe that a person can be given a secure and yet exciting view of his destiny by making an honest investigation of the tested truths of the Bible prophecy. . . .

Some time in the future there will be a seven-year period climaxed by the visible return of Jesus Christ.

Most prophecies which have not yet been fulfilled concern events which will develop shortly before the beginning of and during this seven-year countdown.

The general time of this seven-year period couldn't begin until the Jewish people re-established their nation in their ancient homeland of Palestine.

Keys to the Prophetic Puzzle

A definite international realignment of nations into four spheres of political power had to occur in the same era as this rebirth of Israel. Each sphere of power had to be led by a certain predicted nation and allied with certain other nations. The relationships of all these factors to each other is easily determined by the following clues: first, each one of the four spheres of political power is said to be present and vitally involved with the reborn state of Israel.

Secondly, each one of these spheres of power is a major factor in the final great war called "Armageddon," which is to be triggered by an invasion of the new state of Israel.

Third, each one of these spheres of power will be judged and destroyed for invading the new state of Israel, by the personal return of the Jewish Messiah, Jesus Christ.

It should be obvious that these predicted movements of history are interrelated in their general time of beginning and ending. This is why the prophecies can be pieced together to make a coherent picture, even though the pieces are scattered in small bits throughout the Old and New Testaments. . . .

Israel, the Fuse of Armageddon

What has happened and what is happening right now to Israel is significant in the entire prophetic picture. . . .To be specific about Israel's great significance as a sign of the time, there are three things that were to happen. First, the Jewish nation would be reborn in the land of

Palestine. Secondly, the Jews would repossess old Jerusalem and the sacred sites. Thirdly, they would rebuild their ancient temple of worship upon its historic site. . . .

The Jewish people, after nearly 2,000 years in exile, under relentless persecution, became a nation again on 14 May 1948. . . .

Then came the war on June 1967—the phenomenal Israeli six-day blitz. I was personally puzzled as to the significance of it all until the third day of fighting when Moshe Dayan, the ingenious Israeli general, marched to the wailing wall, the last remnant of the Old Temple, and said, "We have returned to our holiest of holy places, never to leave her again." . . .

The Third Temple

There remains but one more event to completely set the stage of Israel's part in the last great act of her historical drama. This is to rebuild the ancient Temple of worship upon its old site. There is only one place that this Temple can be built, according to the Law of Moses. This is upon Mount Moriah. . . .

There is one major problem barring the construction of a third Temple. That obstacle is the second holiest place of the Moslem faith, the Dome of the Rock. This is believed to be built squarely in the middle of the old temple site.

Obstacle or no obstacle, it is certain that the Temple will be rebuilt. Prophecy demands it. . . .

Tie It All Together

With the Jewish nation reborn in the land of Palestine, ancient Jerusalem once again under total Jewish control for the first time in 2,600 years, and talk of rebuilding the great Temple, the most important prophetic sign of Jesus Christ's soon coming is before us. This has now set the stage for the other predicted signs to develop in history.

THE
LATE
GREAT
PLANET
EARTH

HAL LINDSEY

with
C. C. CARLSON

ZONDERVAN
PUBLISHING HOUSE
OF THE ZONDERVAN CORPORATION
GRAND RAPIDS MICHIGAN 49506

According to Hal Lindsey, *The Late Great Planet Earth* is a book about Bible prophecy.

It is like the key piece of a jigsaw puzzle being found and then having the many adjacent pieces rapidly fall into place. . . .

Russia is a Gog

The new State of Israel will be plagued by a certain pattern of events which has been clearly forecasted.

Shortly after the restoration of the Jews in the land of Israel, an incredible enemy will arise to its "uttermost north." This enemy will be composed of one great nation which will gather around it a number of allies. It is this "Northern Confederacy" that is destined to plunge the world into its final great war which Christ will return to end. . . .

For centuries, long before the current events could have influenced the interpreter's ideas, men have recognized that Ezekiel's prophecy about the northern commander referred to Russia. . . .

What's the Evidence?

Ezekiel describes this northern commander as "Gog, of the land of Magog, the chief prince (or ruler) of Rosh, of Meschech and Tubal" (Ezekial 38:2 Amplified). This gives the ethnic background of this commander and his people. . . .

Gog is the symbolic name of the nation's leader and Magog is his land. He is also the prince of the ancient people who were called Rosh, Meshech, and Tubal. . . .

Wilhelm Gesenius, a great Hebrew scholar of the early nineteenth century, discusses these words in his unsurpassed *Hebrew Lexicon.* "Meshech" he says, "was founder of the Moschi, a barbarous people, who dwelt in the Moschian mountains."[1]

This scholar went on to say that the Greek name, Moschi,[1] derived from the Hebrew name Meshech is the source of the name for *the city of Moscow.* In discussing Tubal he said, "Tubal is the son of Rapheth, founder of the Tivereni, a people dwelling on the Black Sea to the west of Moschi."

Gesenius concludes by saying that these people undoubtedly make up the modern Russian people. . . .

Dr. Gesenius in his *Hebrew Lexicon* says, ". . . Rosh was a designation for the tribes then north of the Taurus Mountains, dwelling in the neighborhood of the Volga."[2]

He concluded that in this name and tribe we have the first historical trace of the Russ or Russian nation. . . .

Where Is the Uttermost North?

The final evidence for identifying this northern commander lies in its geographical location from Israel. . . .

You need only to take a globe to verify this exact geographical fix. There is only one nation to the "uttermost north" of Israel—the U.S.S.R. . . .

What's Your Game, Gog?

We have seen that Russia will arm and equip a vast confederacy. This powerful group of allies will lead an attack on restored Israel. However, Russia and her confederates will be destroyed completely by an act that Israel will acknowledge as being from their God. This act will bring many in Israel to believe in their true Messiah (Ezekiel 38:15 ff.).

The attack upon the Russian confederacy and the resulting conflict will escalate into the last war of the world, involving all nations.

Then it will happen. Christ will return to prevent the annihilation of all mankind. . . .

Rapture—What Rapture?

Christians have a tendency sometimes to toss out words which have no meaning to the non-Christian. Sometimes misunderstood terms provide the red flag an unbeliever needs to turn him from the simple truth of God's Word. "Rapture" may be one of those words. . . .

Someday, a day that only God knows, Jesus Christ is coming to take away all those who believe in Him. He is coming to meet all true believers in the air. Without benefit of science, space suits, or interplanetary rockets, there will be those who will be transported into a glorious place more beautiful, more awesome, than we can possibly comprehend. Earth and all its thrills, excitement, and pleasures will be nothing in contrast to this great event.

It will be the living end. The ultimate trip. . . .

We have been examining the push of world events which the prophets foretold would lead the way to the seven-year countdown before the return of Jesus Christ to earth. The big question is, will you be here during this seven-year countdown? Will you be here during the time of the Tribulation when the Antichrist and the False Prophet are in charge for a time? Will you be here when the world is plagued by mankind's darkest days? . . .

God's Word tells us that there will be one generation of believers who will never know death. These believers will be removed from the earth before the Great Tribulation—before that period of the most ghastly pestilence, bloodshed, and starvation the world has ever known.

Examine the prophecies of this mysterious happening—of the "Rapture." Here is the real hope for the Christian, the "blessed hope" for true believers (Titus 2:13-15).

As we see the circumstances which are coming on the world, this hope gets more blessed all the time. This is the reason we are optimistic about the future. This is the reason that in spite of the headlines, in spite of crisis after crisis in America and throughout the world, in spite of the dark days which will strike terror into the hearts of many, every Christian has the right to be optimistic!...

When will the Rapture occur? We don't know. No one knows. But God knows. However, we believe that according to all the signs, we are in the general time of His coming....

The Beginning of the End

According to the Bible, the Middle East crisis will continue to escalate until it threatens the peace of the whole world. The focus of all nations will be upon this unsolvable and complex problem which keeps bringing the world to the precipice of a thermonuclear holocaust....

The Arab-African confederacy headed by Egypt (King of the South) launches an invasion of Israel. This fatal mistake spells their doom and begins the Armageddon campaign....

Russia and her allies use this occasion to launch an invasion of the Middle East, which Russia has longed to do since the Napoleonic wars. Ezekiel 38 describes the development of this great Russian force, and its plan to attack Israel.... Strategic wealth will cause the Russian bloc to look for an opportunity to invade and conquer Israel, according to Ezekiel....

The Russian bloc will double-cross the Arabs, Egyptians, and Africans, and for a short while conquer the Middle East.... This Russian double-cross of the Arabs is predictable by any astute observer of the Middle East situation today. It is obvious that the Russians are playing games with the Arabs in order to accomplish the old Russian dream of year-round seaports and oil supplies. The Arab leaders think that they can accept Russian loans and supplies without strings, but there are steel cables of conditions behind every Russian ruble given in aid and they are used eventually to pull a country behind the iron curtain....

Nuclear Exchange Begins

Russia, as well as many countries who thought they were secure under the Antichrist's protection, will have fire fall upon them. Once again, this could be a direct judgment from God, or God could allow the various countries to launch a nuclear exchange of ballistic missiles upon each other....

A Bright Spot in the Gloom

As Armageddon begins with the invasion of Israel by the Arabs and the Russian confederacy, and their consequent swift destruction, the greatest period of Jewish conversion to their true Messiah will begin. Ezekiel predicts that the destruction of the great Russian invading force will have a supernatural element to it which will cause great numbers

67

of Jews to see the hand of the Lord in it. Through the miraculous sign of the destruction of this enemy who sought to destroy all Jews they come to see the name of their true God and Messiah, Jesus Christ. . . .

The Greatest Moment

As the battle of Armageddon reaches its awful climax and it appears that all life will be destroyed on earth—in this very moment Jesus Christ will return and save man from self-extinction.

As history races toward this moment, are you afraid or looking with hope for deliverance? The answer should reveal to you your spiritual condition.

One way or another history continues in a certain acceleration toward the return of Christ. Are you ready?. . .

Prelude to Eternity

First, there is the return of Christ at the climax of the greatest war of all time. Second, Christ separates the surviving believers from the surviving unbelievers; the unbelievers will be judged and cast off the earth (Revelation 20:1-6 cf. Matthew 25:41-46). Third, Christ establishes the millennial kingdom and the surviving believers go into it as mortals and repopulate the earth (Revelation 20:11-15; cf. Matthew 25:31-40). Fourth, at the end of a thousand years the unbelieving children rebel, Christ judges them, then He completely changes the old heaven and earth and creates a new one (Revelation 21; Isaiah 65:17; II Peter 3:8-13). This is the ultimate destiny of all persons who are redeemed by Christ. . . .

Polishing the Crystal Ball

The key that would unlock the prophetic book would be the current events that would begin to fit into the predicted pattern. . . . Here, then, are the things that I believe will happen and develop in the near future. . . .

The Religious Scene

In the institutional church, composed of professing Christians who are in many cases not Christian, look for many things to happen:

With increasing frequency the leadership of the denominations will be captured by those who completely reject the historic truths of the Bible and deny doctrines which according to Christ Himself are crucial to believe in order to be a Christian. . . .

There will be unprecedented mergers of denominations into "religious conglomerates.". . .

Young people will continue to accelerate their exodus from the institutional churches. . . .

There will be an ever-widening gap between the true believers in Christ and those who masquerade as "ministers of righteousness.". . . Look for movements within Israel to make Jerusalem the religious center of the world and to rebuild their ancient Temple on its old site.

The Political Scene

Keep your eyes on the Middle East. If this is the time that we believe it is, this area will become a constant source of tension for all the world. . . .

Israel will become fantastically wealthy and influential in the future. Keep your eyes upon the development of riches in the Dead Sea.

The United States will not hold its present position of leadership in the western world; financially, the future leader will be Western Europe. . . .

Look for a growing desire around the world for a man who can govern the entire world.

Look for some limited use of modern nuclear weapons somewhere in the world. . . .This limited use could occur between Russia and China, or upon the continental United States.

The Sociological Scene

Look for the present sociological problems such as crime, riots, lack of employment, poverty, illiteracy, mental illness, illegitimacy, etc., to increase. . .

Look for the beginning of the widest spread famines in the history of the world.

Look for drug addiction to further permeate the U.S. and other free-world countries. . . .

Conclusion

As we see the world becoming more chaotic, we can be "steadfast" and "immovable," because we know where it's going and where we are going. We know that Christ will protect us until His purpose is finished and then He will take us to be with Himself. . . .

---

[1] Wilhelm Gesenius, D.D., *Hebrew and English Lexicon.*

[2] Gesenius.

10 FOREIGN POLICY AND THE MILITARY

THE THEOLOGY
OF NUCLEAR WAR:
THE COUNTERPOINT

Andrew Lang and Fundamentalists Anonymous

Andrew Lang wrote this article in his capacity as the director of the Christic Institute's Armageddon Project, a program of research into the political ideology of the Religious Right in the United States. He is also the editor of Convergence, *the Institute's newsmagazine on politics and religion. The Christic Institute is a nonprofit, nonpartisan center for law and national policy in the public interest.*

Fundamentalists Anonymous was formed in March 1985 to support people who want to free themselves from the fundamentalist mindset and to educate the American public on how the fundamentalist agenda threatens the pluralism and basic liberties of American life. Their comments were reprinted from The FA Networker, *the quarterly support group newsletter of Fundamentalists Anonymous.*

Points to Consider:

1. Summarize what will take place during the Great Tribulation.
2. What does the phrase "nuclearization of the Bible" mean?
3. Describe the Rapture.
4. Explain why fundamentalists do not fear nuclear war.

Andrew Lang, *The Political Eschatology of the Religious Right* (Washington, D.C.: Christic Institute, 1986), pp. 1-4, 8-9.

"Armageddon Theology and the Fundamentalist Mindset," *The FA Networker,* Spring 1987, p. 10.

by Andrew Lang

Introduction

In the history of politics in the United States there have been few mass movements so completely controlled by ideology as the Religious Right. . . .The most visible personalities in this movement agree on eschatology—the doctrine of the end-time. . . .

The most important eschatological system in the Religious Right is "dispensational premillennialism," an historic tradition in fundamentalist and pentecostal Christianity. Today, this tradition is one of the dominant forms—although by no means the only form—of fundamentalism in the United States.[1] Jerry Falwell, Jimmy Swaggart, Tim LaHaye, Oral Roberts, and most of the other political pastors of the Religious Right are dispensationalists. Pat Robertson follows a variant form of premillennialism.

The Great Tribulation

Dispensational premillennialism divides history into stages, or "dispensations," from the creation of humanity to the Second Coming of Christ, and beyond. Each dispensation ends in a violent crisis between man and God. The time in which we live is the final dispensation before the Second Coming, the end-time of human history. It, too, will end in crisis: a seven-year convulsion of global warfare and economic chaos (the "Great Tribulation") reaching a savage climax in the Battle of Armageddon.

Dispensationalists believe that God's "countdown" for human history is spelled out in the Bible. They read the Bible as an infallible history book dictated by the Holy Spirit to prophets and apostles. But it is a history book about the future as well as the past. Consequently, succeeding generations of dispensationalists have searched the daily newspaper for "signs of the times." In the world wars and revolutions of this century, they have seen evidence of the coming end-times chaos described in Bible prophecy. Today, the theorists of Armageddon interpret the rise of Soviet power and the nuclear war danger as key indicators that the Great Tribulation is about to begin.

The Great Tribulation is Satan's last desperate gamble for power. As he seizes control of nations and churches, the world plunges into a war crisis. This crisis precipitates the destruction of political and religious systems, including the Soviet empire.

The deadliest catastrophes of the Tribulation period will center on Israel. Sometime within the next fifty years, Jerry Falwell believes, Soviet forces will invade the Middle East and meet their doom "on the mountains of Israel."[2] This holocaust, he writes, will "purge Israel."[3] The surviving Jews will convert en masse to Christianity. The Soviet Union will be "totally destroyed," either by nuclear weapons or by fire from

71

WHEN WILL THE RAPTURE OCCUR?

There are so many inopportune times the rapture could happen: when you've just sat down, with popcorn and beer, for the Super Bowl; when you're on your first date and all is going smoothly; when you're on your way to confession or the local gospel tent after a long absence; when you've just paid huge bucks for a new house; when your baby is due in a week (Jesus himself mentioned that one). Christians should pray that God won't pick the wrong day.

Michael J. Farrell, National Catholic Reporter, *November 16, 1984*

heaven.[4] Armageddon will be the final catastrophe of this period—a war between Christ and Antichrist fought in Israel on the plain of Esdraelon.

The Great Tribulation is a global purge of atheists and heretics. "The Tribulation will result in such bloodshed and destruction that any war up to that time will seem insignificant," Falwell writes. "There will come a day when God will unleash His wrath and judgment upon unbelievers. He will crush them beneath His thumb.[5]

This worldwide catastrophe will end with the dawning of the Millennium, the Kingdom of God on earth. This is no spiritual kingdom but a political system, an absolute monarchy governed by a ruling class of born-again Christians.[6]

Because all of these events are outlined in Bible prophecy, they constitute God's master plan for history. No government, no arms control treaty can stop the countdown to Armageddon.

Falwell's linkage of nuclear warfare with Bible prophecy underlines the most important change in Armageddon doctrine since World War II: the "nuclearization" of the Bible. After the destruction of Hiroshima and Nagasaki, many dispensationalists transformed biblical images of "fire and brimstone" into prophetic visions of nuclear explosions.

The leading apologist for "nuclear dispensationalism" is author Hal Lindsey. In *The Late Great Planet Earth*, Lindsey speculates that the "fire on Magog" described by the Hebrew prophet Ezekiel could be a prediction that nuclear missiles will annihilate the Soviet Union.[7]

Falwell has drawn similar conclusions. The Bible predicts a Soviet invasion of the Middle East, he told the *Los Angeles Times* in 1981. "And it is at that time when I believe there will be some nuclear holocaust on this earth.... And Russia will be the offender and will be ultimately totally destroyed."[8] In late 1984, however, Falwell apparently changed his mind on Bible prophecy and nuclear war. God will destroy the Soviet

72

Illustration by Don Carlton. Reprinted by permission of the *National Catholic Reporter.*

Union, he declared in a sermon, "not with nuclear power but with divine power."[9]

The Rapture

Despite this ideology of global violence, dispensationalism is fundamentally a religion of *survival,* the religious analogue to secular theories of survivable and winnable nuclear war. No dispensationalist equates the coming wars of the end-time with the extinction of humanity. In fact, the theorists of Armageddon contemplate the future with joy. The Tribulation is only the agonized birth of a new age, a messianic era of peace under the kingship of Jesus Christ.

The leaders of the Religious Right do not fear nuclear war for two reasons: (1) Jesus will return at the end of the Tribulation period, saving humanity from self-destruction, and (2) born-again Christians will escape from the planet *before* the missiles strike. This latter theory—the doctrine of the Rapture—is almost universally accepted by the men who today dominate the Religious Right.[10]

Falwell explains: "Those Christians who are alive when the Lord returns will be caught up to meet the Lord in the air. All of this will take place in a split second and will be a glorious time for all believers. This will, however, be a terrible time of confusion for those who are left on earth."[11]

"Someday, a day that only God knows, Jesus Christ is coming to take away all those who believe in him," Hal Lindsey predicts. "He is coming to meet all true believers in the air. Without benefit of science, space suits, or interplanetary rockets, there will be those who will be transported into a glorious place more beautiful, more awesome, than we can possibly comprehend."[12]

Born-again Christians therefore should not fear "the coming war with Russia," Falwell once told his followers. "If you know the Lord Jesus

Christ as your Savior, none of this should bring fear to your heart, because we're going up in the Rapture before any of it occurs.''[13]

The mass evacuation of born-again Christians is followed by the mass execution of God's enemies. ''Imagine,'' Lindsey writes, ''cities like London, Paris, Tokyo, New York, Los Angeles, Chicago—obliterated!''[14] One third of the human race will be wiped out. J. O. Grooms, an evangelist at Falwell's congregation in Lynchburg, Virginia, puts the Tribulation death toll at 1.5 billion, including 138 million Americans. ''This is not pessimism,'' he observes in a tract published by Falwell's Soul Winning Office. ''These are cold hard facts.''[15]

At the close of the Great Tribulation, the raptured saints will return with Jesus to rule a planet cleansed of homosexuals, secular humanists, and Communists. . . .

---

[1] For a history of dispensational premillenialism in the United States, see Timothy P. Weber, *Living in the Shadow of the Second Coming: American Premillennialism 1875-1982* (Grand Rapids: Zondervan, 1983). An important introduction to contemporary dispensationalism by a theologian of the movement is *Dispensationalism Today* by Charles C. Ryrie (Chicago: Moody Press, 1965). For a sympathetic discussion of the relation between dispensationalism and politics, see Norman L. Geisler, ''A Premillennial View of Law and Government,'' *Bibliotheca Sacra,* July-September 1985, pp. 250-266; or Ed Dobson and Ed Hindson, ''Apocalypse Now: What Fundamentalists Believe About the End of the World,'' *Policy Review,* Fall 1986, pp. 16-22.

[2] Jerry Falwell, *Nuclear War and the Second Coming of Jesus Christ,* (Lynchburg: Old Time Gospel Hour, 1983), p. 22.

[3] Falwell, p. 14.

[4] Interview with Jerry Falwell by Robert Scheer, in ''The Prophet of Worldly Methods,'' *Los Angeles Times,* 4 March 1981.

[5] Falwell, *Nuclear War and the Second Coming of Jesus Christ,* pp. 12, 14.

[6] Herman A. Hoyt, ''Dispensational Premillenialism,'' in *The Meaning of the Millennium: Four Views,* ed. Robert S. Clouse (Downers Grove: InterVarsity Press, 1977), p. 81.

[7] Hal Lindsey, *The Late Great Planet Earth* (New York: Bantam, 1973), p. 150. This is the famous ''Gog-Magog War'' described in Ezekiel 38 and 39. Lindsey's influence in dispensationalist circles should not be underestimated. *The Late Great Planet Earth* has sold more than 20 million copies since 1967, and was listed by *The New York Times* as

the best-selling nonfiction title in the United States between 1970 and 1980.

8 Falwell, *Los Angeles Times.*

9 Falwell, unpublished sermon at Thomas Road Baptist Church broadcast on the Old Time Gospel Hour, 2 December 1984.

10 Robertson is the most important exception. As a "post-tribulationist," he believes the Rapture will occur after the Great Tribulation. Christians therefore will remain on the planet throughout the final catastrophe of the present age. A number of Robertson's supporters are "postmillennialists." This group, historically a small minority in fundamentalist churches, believes that born-again Christians will establish the Millennial Kingdom through a seizure of political and military power. Postmillennialists today are increasingly active in the Religious Right.

11 Falwell, *Nuclear War and the Second Coming of Jesus Christ,* p. 6.

12 Lindsey, p. 126.

13 Falwell, in "Ronald Reagan and the Prophecy of Armageddon," radio documentary, writ. and prod. Joe Cuomo, WBAI Radio, Oct. 1984. Research by Larry Jones.

14 Lindsey, p. 155.

15 J. O. Grooms, *Russia Invades Israel When?* (Lynchburg: Thomas Road Baptist Church, 1983).

by Fundamentalists Anonymous

Consider the following statement of **Jimmy Swaggart**, quoted from a sermon delivered on September 22, 1985:

I wish I could say we will have peace. I believe Armageddon is coming. Armageddon is coming. It is going to be fought in the valley of Megiddo. It's coming. They can sign all the peace treaties they want. They won't do any good. There are dark days coming. The problems of Central America will not be solved. The problems of Europe will not be solved. It's going to get worse. . . . I'm not planning on going through the hell that is coming. The Lord will descend from Heaven with a shout. My Lord! I'm happy about it! He's coming again. I don't care who it bothers. I don't care who it troubles. It thrills my soul.

Armageddon Theology

Fundamentalist (including charismatic and Pentacostal) congregations around the country are involved, in one way or another, with Armageddon theology. Certainly the idea of the Second Coming is not always dangerous. But in the hands of a Jimmy Swaggart, Jerry Falwell, or Pat Robertson, the idea of Armageddon becomes part and parcel of the fundamentalist mindset. It creeps into the way fundamentalists view everyday life and world events. Look again at the above statement by Jimmy Swaggart. The central message is that Armageddon is coming immediately, that it could happen tomorrow. In addition to the horrifying prospect that the world could end any day, Swaggart tells us, in effect, that any peace initiatives are futile, that there is no way to change things, that we might as well welcome the destruction. All of the world's problems are inevitable. Everything is going according to plan. Everything follows a script.

This idea that everything is following a script is the most tragic effect of the fundamentalist mindset. If a person believes that the Bible is the literal truth and contains the literal blueprint of the course of history, he or she will feel no inclination to attempt to change the course of events. If all of the problems of Africa, Central America, and Europe were forseen in the Book of Ezekiel, there is no point in trying to make things better. When Armageddon theology works itself into the fundamentalist mindset, the result is the ultimate denial of responsibility. Believers are urged by their ministers to sit back and let history go by, let the world take its course—even if that course will eventually knock it off its axis.

Developing nuclear weapons was a part of God's plan. Nuclear war may be the fulfillment of (Biblical) prophecy.

—**Edward A. McAteer,** Executive Director, The Religious Roundtable

A Defeatist Message

When Armageddon theology takes root, it teaches that life is worthless. The here and now of day-to-day life is ignored. The message of Jimmy Swaggert and all who preach Armageddon theology is an essentially defeatist message.

After all, people caught in the fundamentalist mindset have tunnel vision. They look only at a future when the saved will be raptured and not have to deal with all the individual and social troubles that come with being human. They don't see what's around them, but only the light at the end. If the walls of the tunnel begin to crumble, they won't care.

Armageddon theology is the last step of the fundamentalist mindset. It is the logical outcome of a system of thought which tells people not to think or act for themselves. Just as men and women in fundamentalist churches are told not to doubt or ask questions, they are told not to worry about or act to combat the problems facing the entire world. War, violence, death, and destruction are all foretold in the Bible. Therefore, according to the mindset, they are part of God's plan, and to stand against them is to stand against God.

Here is what we can expect to happen in the days, months, and years ahead. Having been regathered from the countries of the world, Israel, a unified nation living in relative security, will be invaded by a confederation from the north and the east. Indications are that this great power from the north may be the Soviet Union, for that nation occupies land specified by Ezekiel.

—**Pat Robertson,** *The Secret Kingdom* (1984, Bantam Books), p. 213

Fundamentalists as World Leaders

Europeans in the 10th century thought the world was going to end in the year 1000. People walked around the countryside whipping one another. Today, the doomsayers have more effective weapons than whips.

Jimmy Swaggart doesn't care who it bothers. He doesn't care who it troubles. He has thrown his support behind Pat Robertson's "exploration" of the Presidency. Do we want to be led by people who don't care? Do we want our leaders to follow a vision which, in anticipation of the final days, prevents them from devoting all their energies to attempting to resolve current world problems? Will we allow the end of the world to thrill *our* souls? Who are *they* to tell us that peace isn't worth struggling for! How *dare* they presume to use religious belief to tell us that life in the here and now is hopeless and worthless!

11 FOREIGN POLICY AND THE MILITARY

THE MARXIST THREAT IN NICARAGUA

Casey Dolan

Casey Dolan is the pseudonym of a woman who has extensive contacts in the political community in the U.S. and in Latin America. Her article appeared in The Wanderer, *a conservative, national Catholic weekly.*

Points to Consider:

1. Describe the present conditions in Nicaragua.
2. Why did Nicaraguan minister of the interior Tomas Borge refer to American visitors as "an army of useful fools"?
3. Define turbas divinas and explain their role in the Nicaraguan government.
4. According to this author, what would happen if Nicaragua became a Soviet base?

Casey Dolan, "Crucial Reports on Nicaragua Ignored," *The Wanderer,* June 18, 1987, p. 3.

Using Nicaragua as a base, the Soviets and Cubans can become the dominant power in the crucial corridor between North and South America.

Amid the still swirling controversy of the Iran-*contra* affair, Congress has begun debate on the continuing aid to the Nicaraguan *contras.* Both print and broadcast media have bombarded the public with reams of information on the issue of *contra*-gate, continuing to cast suspicion on key government figures, especially the President himself.

The President's Warning

In the light of such adverse publicity many will dismiss as mere rhetoric or at best a political maneuver, President Reagan's appeal to members of Congress: "If we cut off the freedom fighters, we will be giving the Soviets a free hand in Central America."

The President made the appeal on May 3 in New York City before 2,000 or more members of the American Publishers' Association. It was more than an appeal. It was a warning to the entire American nation.

A Threat to National Security

What should disturb every American is the failure of the press to present a balanced picture of existing conditions in Central America. As early as 1981, Daniel Ortega told his subordinates: "Our doctrine is Marxism-Leninism." Proof of the link between Daniel Ortega, Castro, and the Soviet Union exists in a staggering amount of documentation available from the Office of Public Diplomacy for Latin America and the Caribbean in the State Department.

These documents focus on every aspect of present conditions in Nicaragua and graphically portray the Sandinista government as a potential threat to the entire Caribbean region. What most Americans do not realize is that our sea lanes converge in the Caribbean. These involve 45 percent of our imports and exports, over 60 percent of NATO supplies and 55 percent of our crude oil imports. The Soviets, however, are well aware of the strategic advantage control of this area could give them. Pressure on us by the Soviets aligned with Cuba and Nicaragua would force us to focus our attention on an area we once thought posed no threat to our national security.

A Soviet Buildup

This diversionary tactic on the part of the Soviets with the help of Nicaragua and Cuba would pin us down and enable Soviet leaders to expand in other parts of the world without fear of interference from the United States.

Proof of the Soviet buildup in Nicaragua is substantial in an excess
of State Department documents containing photographs of military in-
stallations and weaponry, graphs, and statistics reinforced with well-
documented textual material. The documents speak for themselves.

An Army of "Useful Fools"

Documentation also exists to support the charge that Nicaragua is
actively involved with the Soviet Union in supplying Communist guer-
rillas in other Central American countries with the weaponry needed
to destabilize and ultimately conquer the whole Caribbean region.

Yet the Sandinistas have spared nothing in their effort to create the
illusion that the people of Nicaragua live in a free society, posing no
threat to their Central American neighbors. The Nicaraguan minister
of the interior, Tomas Borge, who is behind the guided tours of
Nicaragua, has conducted his campaign of disinformation so well many
visitors are blinded to the reality of Marxism-Leninism which he so art-
fully conceals. Defectors from the Sandinista camp as well as victims
of its oppression paint a very different picture from the one that visitors
see.

Lt. Alvaro Baldizon, a defector who served as chief investigator for
Borge, has testified that the minister of the interior refers to American
visitors who believe him as "an army of useful fools." Baldizon gave
testimony before the House Subcommittee on Human Rights on Oct.
9, 1985. When asked about human rights violations by the *contras* he
said from what he had seen, the *contras* did not have a policy of human
rights abuses that the Sandinistas did. The State Department document
Inside Nicaragua: A Special Investigator's Perspective, printed in 1986,
contains a wealth of information about the Sandinistas' attempt to
deceive the free world with regard to their treatment of the Nicaraguan
people.

The Divine Mobs

Documents smuggled out by Baldizon when he escaped from Nicaragua, some of which appear in this report, provide proof of assassinations of opponents of the Sandinista regime with the full knowledge of the Nicaraguan government. He has confirmed that it regularly uses murder and torture to control opposition and trains the *turbas divinas* (the divine mobs) composed of toughs and criminals as civilian shock troops to break up demonstrations. Using tactics such as stoning and beating with clubs, vandalizing houses and burning vehicles, they are an effective deterrent to any open government opposition.

Baldizon supplied this information in extensive debriefings by U.S. government officials and in testimony before members of Congress and the press.

Information Gap Exists

A most recent report from the State Department, *Human Rights in Nicaragua Under the Sandinistas, From Revolution to Repression* has presented far more extensive and irrefutable evidence of the attempt of the Sandinistas to impose their Communist ideology on the people of Nicaragua. Prime targets for repression are the press and both the

Catholic and Protestant Churches. Documentation substantiates the charges made by men like the exiled Bishop Vega, that repression of organized religion is on the increase. So are the attacks on those who exercise freedom of speech either in the press or through the private sector.

This latest document, over 250 pages in length, leaves no doubt that the Sandinistas have been brutal and cruel in their attempt to suppress the basic civil and religious rights of the Nicaraguan people. This is the Nicaragua that visitors never see, that the American press working in a free society has chosen to suppress in its reports on the struggle of the *contras*. Equally remiss are the staffers in congressional offices in both the House and the Senate, all of whom have access to this material. Members of Congress must certainly assume some of the responsibility for the information gap they have helped to create and the confusion they have caused. Many will find it difficult to believe that such a media blackout does, in fact, exist.

Continue Aid to *Contras*

Readers of this article are urged to obtain the comprehensive report, *The Challenge to Democracy in Central America,* issued by the State Department. Set in *Newsweek* format, complete with photographs, graphs, and documented text, this issue gives an overview of Nicaragua (and its Central American neighbors) and proves conclusively that it now serves the interest of the Soviet Union and Cuba. Soviet expansion in the area is real and poses a serious threat to the national security of the whole Western Hemisphere.

While in North Korea in June 1980, Tomas Borge made this statement: "The Nicaraguan revolutionaries will not be content until the imperialists have been overthrown in all parts of the world. . . .We stand with the. . .socialist countries." Anyone reading this report alone can only be horrified by the magnitude of the threat the Nicaraguan buildup poses to the whole of the Caribbean region, not to mention the danger it creates on our southern flank. This is inevitable if aid to the *contras* is stopped and the Sandinista aggression escalates to the point where it engulfs all of Central America.

Nicaragua: A Soviet Base

We should take President Reagan's warning seriously. In his address to the nation, March 16, 1986, he warned: "Using Nicaragua as a base, the Soviets and Cubans can become the dominant power in the crucial corridor between North and South America. Established there, they will be in a position to threaten the Panama Canal, interdict our vital Caribbean sea lanes, and ultimately move against Mexico. Should that happen, desperate Latin peoples by the millions would begin fleeing north into the cities of the southern United States, or to wherever some hope of freedom remained." What President Reagan did not say he implied.

But Tomas Jorge said it for him when he threatened: "The Nicaraguan revolutionaries will not be content until the imperialists have been overthrown in all parts of the world. . . ."

If Central America falls, we will be left in isolation, waiting helplessly until, in turn, we too, are forced to make the choice already made by the freedom fighters in Nicaragua: to stand and fight or to slip wordlessly under the domination of the red flag of tyranny. What is needed and desperately is a massive mobilization of grassroots activists, armed with the above information to write our representatives in Congress demanding aid for the freedom fighters.

FOREIGN POLICY
AND THE MILITARY

THE AMERICAN THREAT
IN NICARAGUA

Robert McAfee Brown

*Robert McAfee Brown is a Protestant theologian and the author of
many books, including* Saying Yes and Saying No: On Rendering to
God and Caesar, *a book in whlch Dr. Brown confronts the dilemma
that exists when official government policies seem to clash with ideas
about God's kingdom of peace and justice. Dr. Brown wrote* Saying
Yes and Saying No *in his capacity as Professor Emeritus of Theology
and Ethics at Pacific School of Religion in Berkeley, California.*

Points to Consider:

1. Describe the conditions of the Nicaraguan people under the Somoza
   dictatorship.
2. Explain what the author means by the double standard that confuses specks and logs.
3. How does Dr. Brown's assessment of the contras contrast with President Reagan's definition?
4. Summarize Dr. Brown's three methods of saying "No" to the
   government.

Robert McAfee Brown, *Saying Yes and Saying No: On Rendering to
God and Caesar* (Philadelphia: The Westminister Press, 1986), pp.
83-94. Reprinted from *Saying Yes and Saying No,* by Robert McAfee
Brown. Copyright © 1986 Robert McAfee Brown. Used by permission
of The Westminister Press.

Unless our nation forgoes its disastrous decision to use military means to solve political problems in Central America, there will be an escalating double tragedy: the tragedy of the further killing of Nicaragua's peasants by terrorists acting in our name and with our blessing, and the tragedy of our great nation increasingly locked into the consequences of an ideological obsession that bears almost no relation to reality.

Background Information

There have already been many casualties in Nicaragua, and by the time this appears in print there will have been many more. The worst casualties, of course, have been sustained by the Nicaraguan people themselves. Forty-two years under the ruthless dictatorship of the Somoza family (kept in power by successive United States Republican and Democratic administrations) took a terrible toll: imprisonments, torture, disappearances, firing squads, informers; not to mention economic deprivation, as the Somoza family brazenly took land and money from the already poor. (When the Somozas were finally toppled, their landholdings had become so extensive that if their land had been distributed to the peasants, each one would have received more than five acres.)

When this situation finally became intolerable, there was a popular uprising in which the Somozas were defeated and fled (with all their millions) to Miami and elsewhere. Before leaving, however, they completed the devastation of their country by killing thousands of those in rebellion and systematically blowing up all the factories, office buildings, and other construction they could.

Consequently, when the Sandinistas (a coalition of many groups— left, right, and center) assumed power in July 1979, the cities and countryside they inherited were devastated by civil war, the population was decimated, the people were war-weary, and the country was desperately poor, without significant resources for rebuilding.

Largely because of the enmity of the United States things have not only remained that way but gotten worse. By *military* means (giving military supplies to antigovernment guerilla groups that engage in border raids on civilians, and building up a massive military presence in Central America; by *economic* means (imposing a trade embargo that makes it illegal for U.S. business interests to trade with Nicaragua); by *political* means (seeking to line up other nations against Nicaragua); by *illegal* means (mining Nicaraguan harbors in violation of international law and issuing manuals urging the murder of Nicaraguan political leaders); and by every other means at its disposal, our administration has sought to crush Nicaragua (make it "say uncle" is the phrase Mr. Reagan uses)—a country that wishes to build its future free from the

> *Fundamentalists have pressured our government to give support to the Contras in Nicaragua. They've also privately funded the Contra rebels.*
>
> Fundamentalists Anonymous, January 1987

control of any outside nation, whether the USA or the USSR. In the process of doing all of this, the administration has created another casualty in addition to the Nicaraguan peasants. That casualty is truth.

Why has the administration done this? It has decided that Nicaragua is a Russian satellite, that it represents the tentacles of Moscow reaching into "our continent" (as former Defense Secretary Weinberger liked to call it), and that all means that will unite the American people around Nicaragua's destruction are appropriate.

The administration's claim that this poverty-stricken nation's three million inhabitants are plotting to destroy the United States is not shared by most of the rest of the world, so the United States is increasingly isolated in its anti-Nicaraguan posture. . . .

What we need is an understanding of the ways in which our leaders manipulate the truth to support their claims. We do not have the moral privilege of remaining silent when truth is a casualty. . . .

Five Ways to Make Truth a Casualty
(With Extensive Help From the United States Government)

1. *The double standard that confuses specks and logs.* We are warned in the Sermon on the Mount that we should first take the log out of our own eye before seeking to remove a speck from someone else's eye (Matt. 7:3-5). That is always good advice, but the admonition can be pressed even further in relation to our government's treatment of Nicaragua. For while it never occurs to the administration that it might have a log in its own eye, it is continually engaging in a microscopic examination of Nicaragua's presumed sins in order to magnify specks into logs, while ignoring or minimizing the massively visible sins of other nations (usually nations we support) so that their logs shrink to the size of specks. And whenever this happens, truth becomes a casualty. . . . For example, while supporting the terrorist regime of Marcos in the Philippines (whom both Secretary of State Shultz and Vice-President Bush have commended for significant progress in the achievement of human rights) and the terrorist regime of Pinochet in Chile (which the United States helped to bring to power and whose repressive measures

In Saying Yes and Saying No: On Rendering to God and Caesar, Robert McAfee Brown confronts the dilemma that exists when official government policies seem to clash with ideas about God's kingdom of peace and justice.

it has supported for over a decade), the administration works for the outright overthrow—not reform—of the government of Nicaragua, whose record of human rights is infinitely superior to that of either the Philippines or Chile. A double standard.

2. The undocumented statement that turns out to be false. One reason the administration can employ the double standard so effectively is that it bases its assessment of Nicaragua on undocumented statements that turn out, upon examination, to be false. A refinement of this position, also widely employed by the administration, is to make so-called "documented statements" in which the documentation itself turns out to be false. . . . For example the State Department leaked a report that a shipment going from Russia to Nicaragua contained MIG warplanes, and the report was used for a full week to arouse anti-Nicaragua sentiment in the United States. When the shipment arrived and was unloaded, it contained no MIGs. In another instance, the administration announced that the Nicaraguan government had just started building a new airport with runways designed to accommodate Russian bombers. A former U.S. military official pointed out that work on the airport had begun under the Somoza regime and had nothing to do with Russian bombers. . . .

3. The self-fulfilling prophecy that puts small truths at the service of big lies. One of the most effective ways of making a casualty of truth is to create a self-fulfilling prophecy, in which a small fact that by itself may be true is presented in such a way that its truth communicates a lie. The administration's self-fulfilling prophecy is usually some variant of the theme, "Nicaragua is developing closer and closer ties with Russia, just as we predicted." What is not stated is that to the degree that this is true, it is often due to the actions of the United States.

For instance, it is true that Daniel Ortega, the president of Nicaragua, went to Moscow in the spring of 1985 (as well as to a number of other countries), where he arranged for shipments of farm machinery, grain, and other agricultural necessities—a clear indication, according to our administration, of increasing dependence on Russia. But it is also true that several months earlier Nicaragua had applied to the Inter-American Development Bank for a $58,000,000 loan to purchase the same kind of agricultural equipment and that Secretary of State Shultz (in an almost unprecedented move) had intervened to urge that the loan be denied. Unable to get help from the bank, Mr. Ortega had little recourse but to turn elsewhere. A self-fulfilling prophecy was created by Mr. Schulz's action. . . .

4. The extravagant rhetoric that sees reality in reverse. The above devices for making a casualty of truth are strengthened when highly placed officials make statements about Nicaragua that are patently false and repeat them frequently enough so that listeners will begin to assume they must be true. (In dictatorships, this technique is called "The Big Lie.") An unintended result of this device is that the truth can often be discovered by believing the opposite of what the government official says.

For example, Mr. Reagan consistently refers to the Nicaraguan government as "terrorist" and the country as a "terrorist jungle." At the same time he refers to the U.S.-backed *contras,* who are trying to destroy the government, as "freedom fighters," often likening them to our own "founding fathers." The truth of the matter is the reverse: if we are going to employ rhetoric about "terrorists" at all, it is the U.S.-backed *contras* on whom the title must be bestowed. There are hundreds of documented cases, compiled by international teams of observers, of the terrorist activities of the *contras,* who sweep over the border from Honduras, murder civilians, rape women, kidnap children, burn crops, destroy granaries and warehouses, and attack hospitals and child care centers. To the degree that there are "terrorists" in Nicaragua, they are almost exclusively terrorists who have been funded, supported, and trained by the United States. If the *contras* truly represent our "founding fathers," they represent a chapter in our own history of which we can only be ashamed.

5. The demonic assertion that we alone are not subject to the truth. The worst casualty to truth comes after it has been so manipulated that the manipulators can redefine it to suit their own ends. . . .There is a clear example of this in our relations with Nicaragua. The United States has engaged in many illegal activities in Nicaragua, such as blowing up oil refineries near the coast, but none has been more blatant than its mining of Nicaraguan harbors in an effort to scare off ships trading with Nicaragua. Such action is illegal under international law, and our government knows it. After unsuccessful attempts to deny the mining by blaming it on "independent" *contra* forces, the United States had to acknowledge responsibility for the action.

That is bad enough, but what is even worse is that when the Nicaraguan government quite rightly responded by appealing to the World Court for a judgment against the United States in this matter, the Reagan administration decided that rather than subject itself to international law or acknowledge the constraint of truth, it would refuse to do either. So in an act of disdain for truth, the administration responded by announcing that for the next two years it would refuse to recognize the jurisdiction of the World Court in any matters pertaining to Central America. The truth would be that *whatever the United States wished to do it would do,* and that it would not consider itself answerable to anyone else. Truth would be determined by no body of world opinion, no World Court, only at the whim of what was convenient for the administration.

The fact that the administration's heavy-handed decision to thumb its nose at international law has engendered so little domestic protest is itself a symptom of how deeply the sickness has invaded our entire society. . . .

The Necessity of Saying No

If there is a single point at which, in commitment to the God of Justice, we must say No to the false god of national idolatry, it is surely in relation to the matter now under discussion. For without that No, truth is not only a casualty but a casualty that may have little hope of recovery. When lies become official policy, truth has a hard time making a comeback. How can we say No effectively?

First, we can insist on a distinction between our country and the government. . . . . Let us never concede that because people have been elected to public office they are exempt from challenge and critique; on the contrary, they are more than ever subject to challenge and critique, because they now speak and act not just for themselves but for all of us; what they say and do on our behalf is something for which we can be held morally accountable.

We can make a *second* distinction, this time between the executive and legislative branches of government. In the case of Nicaragua, it has been the executive branch, the White House, that has initiated most of the policies designed to destroy the Nicaraguan government. For a long time it was the legislative branch, the Congress, that ensured whatever restraint remained in our policy. But in May 1985, the backbone of Congress melted, which left the way open for the White House to engage in an increasingly unfettered policy of destruction. . . .

Unless our nation forgoes its disastrous decision to use military means to solve political problems in Central America, there will be an escalating double tragedy: the tragedy of the further killing of Nicaragua's peasants by terrorists acting in our name and with our blessing, and the tragedy of our great nation increasingly locked into the consequences of an ideological obsession that bears almost no relation to reality.

A *third* way of saying No to the government is saying Yes to forces trying to create an alternative policy. . . . Witness for Peace has sent hundreds of United States citizens to Nicaragua to embody a nonviolent presence of solidarity with Nicaraguans. Often staying in the dangerous northern border areas, members of Witness for Peace say, in effect, "We are willing to share with you the physical danger of the *contra* raids, to tell you and the world that there are U.S. citizens who want to support you with hands of helping rather than destroy you with arms of death." Such visitations also expose more and more U.S. citizens to the realities of Nicaraguan life in contrast to the fantasies of administration rhetoric. . . .

It is sad that people must be pushed to such measures in an attempt to be faithful to the God of justice. But only in this way will the modern Caesars realize that they are playing a losing game, even by their standards, and begin to respond to the best instincts of the people of the

United States rather than imposing their own worst instincts on the people of Nicaragua.

13

FOREIGN POLICY
AND THE MILITARY

NUCLEAR FREEZE:
BETRAYING THE NATION

David A. Noebel, Wayne C. Lutton, and Jay Butler

This reading was excerpted from a pamphlet titled War, Peace, and the Nuclear Freeze. *The authors of the pamphlet are described below.*

Dr. David A. Noebel wrote this pamphlet in his capacity as the president of Summit Ministries and was educated at Milwaukee Bible College, Hope College (B.A.), University of Tulsa (M.A.), and the University of Wisconsin (Ph.D. candidate in philosophy).

Dr. Wayne C. Lutton wrote this pamphlet in his capacity as a professor at Summit Ministries and was educated at Bradley University (B.A.), University of South Carolina (M.A.), and Southern Illinois University (Ph.D. degree in history).

Rev. Jay Butler wrote this pamphlet in his capacity as a professor at Summit Ministries and was educated at American Christian College (B.A.) and Dallas Theological Seminary (Th.M. degree in Old Testament).

Points to Consider:

1. Compare and contrast the responsibilities of the church, the home, and the state.
2. How do the Communists define "peace"?
3. Describe the moral alternative to the nuclear freeze.
4. Summarize the authors' view regarding the arms race and nuclear war.

David A. Noebel, Wayne C. Lutton, and Jay Butler, *War, Peace, and the Nuclear Freeze* (Manitou Springs, Co.: Summit Press, 1984), pp. 1-3, 23-25.

The freeze offers no real hope of averting the threat of nuclear war or nuclear blackmail. It may be a pacifist's dream, but it is a Christian realist's nightmare.

After reading *Nuclear Holocaust and Christian Hope* by Dr. Ronald J. Sider and Richard K. Taylor, *Christ and Violence* by Sider, *Preaching on Peace* by Sider and Darrell J. Brubaker, *Waging Peace* edited by Jim Wallis, the U.S. Catholic Bishops letter *The Challenge of Peace: God's Promise and Our Response,* John H. Yoder's *The Politics of Jesus,* Guy F. Hershberger's *War, Peace and Nonresistance,* Edward M. Kennedy and Mark O. Hatfield's *Freeze! How You Can Help Prevent Nuclear War* and scores of other books and articles it is necessary and timely to present the Christian public a more balanced approach to nuclear weaponry, and especially a balanced view regarding the Bible, peace, and pacifism.

Is the Bible a Handbook on Pacifism?

Dr. Ronald J. Sider, a major pacifist, has called upon America to discard both her nuclear and conventional weapons. Is this the true Biblical, spiritual, loving Christian position? Is the Bible a handbook on pacifism? Was Jesus a pacifist? Does following Jesus entail pacifism? Sider, among others, say "yes." We believe a deeper understanding of Scripture says "no."

"Blessed are the peacemakers"; "resist not evil"; "Whosoever shall smite thee on the right cheek, turn to him the other also"; and "Love your enemies" of Matthew 5 is the pacifism of the church. As such it has little to do with the other two equally God-ordained institutions, namely, the home and the state.

The Home and the State

God ordained the home to protect, provide for, and perpetuate the family. God planned for the physically stronger male to protect his wife and children.

God likewise ordained the state to protect its citizens and to execute wrath upon the evildoer. It is not the responsibility of the church to maintain law and order. The church doesn't have the necessary and sufficient means to incarcerate the rapist and the murderer. The church's tools are moral and spiritual principles and sanctions.

The moral responsibility to execute punishment upon the murderer is the state's responsibility. And nothing Jesus said in Matthew 5 negates the state's function or role in society. The Bible doesn't teach anarchy.

A PROPHECY PACKET

In 1983 Jerry Falwell attacked the nuclear freeze movement with a "prophecy packet" (two tapes and a pamphlet) entitled "Nuclear War and the Second Coming of Christ." As Falwell states in his pamphlet, "the one brings thoughts of fear, destruction, and death while the other brings thoughts of joy, hope, and life. They almost seem inconsistent with one another. Yet, they are indelibly intertwined." Falwell, like many of his fellow dispensationalists, believes he will be raptured before nuclear war breaks out.

Larry Kickman, Covert Action Information Bulletin, *Spring 1987*

Michael Novak* said, "Long ago, St. Augustine wished that human beings were reasonable, pacific, and brotherly. Seeing that, instead, passion regularly darkens human minds and evil governs human hearts, he realized that every peace between nations must be built upon a balance of military power. He realized that it is fear of armed might, not reason, that induces nations to negotiate. In an evil world, force is reason's daily instrument. Force without justice is brutal; justice without force is vain."

The Pacifists' Flaw

The pacifists' fatal flaw is confusing God's charge to the church with God's charge to the state. The state, like the church and home, is an institution established by God for the specific purpose of protecting the weak and innocent and executing judgment upon the guilty. Jesus never once suggested to a soldier that he desert his uniform or drop out of service. No other Biblical writer did either. Jesus charged Peter to "put up his sword" because Peter was not the sheriff. The church was never called to advance its teachings or lifestyles by the sword. But government was ordained by God to punish the evil one, to make the way of the transgressor hard, and to protect the weak and the innocent. This truth runs from Genesis 9:6 through Romans 13:1-4 and on to Revelation 19.

---

*Editor's note: Michael Novak is a contemporary Catholic theologian and a prominent national spokesman for conservative political causes.

Illustration by Susan Harlan. Copyright 1983, *USA Today*. Reprinted with permission.

Carl F. H. Henry* said in his *God, Revelation and Authority* (Volume IV, p. 537): "Jesus' role as Messiah on the one hand preserves the divinely established orders—including that of government—as a larger context within which the church carries on her witness in the age of grace."

The Nuclear Freeze Issue

Some are using the nuclear freeze issue as an excuse to advocate total unilateral disarmament. Others are using the freeze issue as an excuse to freeze American citizens in fear thus destroying their will to resist a major communist "peace" offensive. Still others are displaying their total dishonesty in not demanding a freeze when the forces of the USA and the USSR were equal (1969/70). Instead, they waited until the USA decided to narrow the gap that had grown in the 1970s and early 80s, and the Soviets decided to launch their deceptive "peace" offensive!

Unfortunately, many sincere peace groups and pacifists are seconding the communist "peace" offensive never realizing that the communist usage of the term "peace" simply means cessation of effort to stop

---

*Editor's note: Carl F. H. Henry is a theological spokesman for the Religious Right.

communist advances. From a communist point of view there will only be peace when there is no opposition to communism. Some U.S. churches (namely, Riverside Church of New York) which continue to parallel the communist "peace" line, are not only betraying their country, but their Lord.

Our position is quite similar to the French Catholic bishops in their work *Win the Peace*. "Does a country that is threatened in its existence, its liberty, or its identity have a moral right to meet threat with effective counter-threat, even if that counter-threat is nuclear?" The bishops answered, "yes."

We know from the Bible that we are not to be misled by those who speak "peace" to their neighbor, but mischief is in their heart (Psalms 28:3). We also know from the Bible that only when the Prince of Peace, the Lord Jesus Christ, reigns as King of Kings and Lord of Lords will there be genuine and lasting peace on the earth. In the meantime, we must secure the peace as best we can by: (a) establishing inner peace of the heart through spiritual and moral conversion, and (b) segregation and punishment of evildoers who cry peace, peace, while gulag is on their mind and rebellion against God's order is praxis. . . .

Is There a Moral Alternative to the Nuclear Freeze?

The United States can use its technological superiority and experience in space to build a comprehensive non-nuclear, space-based defense system that can destroy incoming Soviet missiles, but does not threaten any people with annihilation. Such a system could be deployed within a relatively short time (the ground-based point defense of our missile silos could commence soon after Congress appropriated the funds) and at modest cost—approximately $5-6 billion per year for about ten years, an amount less than the federal government annually gives away in foreign aid. This new strategy, known as High Frontier,* would move us away from the dangerous policy of Mutual Assured Destruction, and the debilitating "balance of terror" to one of Mutual Assured Survival.

Not only can the High Frontier defense system be initially launched using off-the-shelf technology, but as recently as March 15, 1984, Dr. George Keyworth, President Ronald Reagan's science adviser, revealed some important scientific breakthroughs regarding a defensive missile shield and a role that particle beams, lasers, and high-speed computers will play in such a shield. Besides, the continuing development of space that this program will encourage holds promise of enormous industrial, commercial, and energy benefits for all mankind.

---

*Editor's note: This space-based defense system has also been popularly referred to as the "Star Wars" program.

This exciting opportunity for peace with freedom does not require Soviet compliance or trust in unsure verification procedures. The High Frontier concept is concisely explained by General Daniel O. Graham in his book *We Must Defend America: A New Strategy for National Survival.*

On March 23, 1983, President Ronald Reagan addressed the nation on the topic of national security, and said, "Let me share with you a vision of the future which offers hope. It is that we embark on a program to counter the awesome Soviet missile threat with measures that are defensive...what if free people could live secure in the knowledge that their security did not rest upon the threat of instant U.S. retaliation to deter a Soviet attack; that we could intercept and destroy strategic ballistic missiles before they reached our own soil or that of our allies? Would it not be better to save lives than to avenge them? We are launching an effort which holds the promise of changing the course of history. There will be risks, and results take time. But with your support, I believe we can do it."

It is clear that a viable, moral alternative to the freeze is available. The freeze offers no real hope of averting the threat of nuclear war or nuclear blackmail. It may be a pacifist's dream, but it is a Christian realist's nightmare. High Frontier offers the Christian a balanced alternative in a nuclear age.

Conclusion

As Christians we do not have to submit to nuclear fear. The Bible nowhere states that man will destroy the earth and all life with it. Neither do we have to resign ourselves to an uncontrolled arms race or an inevitable nuclear war.

The price of peace, however, is still eternal vigilance. Not only do we need a knowledge of what we believe in as free people, but also a knowledge of the Marxist/Leninist worldview. Not only do we need the will to survive, but the courage to apply our knowledge and will toward a workable defense system that incorporates space-age technology and averts the threat posed by the Kremlin's military might and the necessity of arms control agreements which rely upon the good faith of the communists.

Free men should proceed without delay with a Manhattan Project approach that will ultimately render massive nuclear weapons obsolete. If King Uzziah had "cunning men" able to invent engines to shoot arrows and great stones to protect Jerusalem, certainly the United States has such men to protect our nation.

Christians can be active peacemakers as well as passive non-resisters. They should opt for active peacemaking in this fallen world.

FOREIGN POLICY
AND THE MILITARY

NUCLEAR FREEZE:
UPHOLDING SPIRITUAL VALUES

Ronald Sider and Richard Taylor

Ronald Sider studied history and theology at Yale University and received the Ph.D. from that institution in 1969. He co-authored Nuclear Holocaust & Christian Hope *in his capacity as associate professor of theology at Eastern Baptist Theological Seminary and president of Evangelicals for Social Action. In addition, he is convenor of the Unit on Ethics and Society of the Theological Commission of the World Evangelical Fellowship and a member of the board of Bread for the World. He is also the author and editor of several books.*

Richard Taylor studied at Yale Divinity School and Cornell University, and completed a masters degree in social work at Bryn Mawr College in 1962. He co-authored Nuclear Holocaust & Christian Hope *in his capacity as a consultant on outreach and peace ministries for the Sojourners Community and Evangelicals for Social Action. He is also the author of several books.*

Points to Consider:

1. Describe the early church's attitude toward war.
2. Summarize the difficulties one might encounter when working for nuclear disarmament.
3. Why do the authors favor a nuclear freeze?
4. What is a nonmilitary defense? How would it work?

Ronald Sider and Richard Taylor, *Nuclear Holocaust & Christian Hope: A Book for Christian Peacemakers* (Downers Grove, IL: InterVarsity Press, 1982). Taken from Nuclear Holocaust and Christian Hope by Ronald J. Sider and Richard K. Taylor. Used by permission of InterVarsity Press, P.O. Box 1400, Downers Grove, IL 60515.

The freeze idea has enormous advantages as a disarmament proposal. It stops the spiral. It hits the brakes. It gets both sides to stop. It starts to reduce the enormous tensions between the superpowers and therefore reduces the risk of war.

Christians and Nuclear War

How should Christians respond to the growing danger of nuclear war? Is there a word from God for us who live in the most dangerous decade in the history of planet Earth?

Nuclear war is new, but war itself is as old as history. Over the centuries, Christians have responded to the evil of war in two major ways. A minority have believed that Christians ought never to participate in lethal violence. The majority have assumed a "just war" stance, asserting that although war is always horrible it may sometimes be the lesser of two evils. Criteria which have developed over many centuries of careful reflection enable Christians to judge whether a particular war is just or unjust.

Both the authors belong to the first tradition. But we have the deepest respect for Christians taking the just war position. Christians equally committed to Christ and the authority of Scripture disagree on the question of war.

Disagreement over the validity of conventional warfare, however, should not conceal one exceedingly important development. Christians from both traditions are coming to the same conclusion about nuclear war. Whether one begins as a Christian in the just war tradition or as a Christian in the nonviolence tradition, the judgment about nuclear war is the same. . . .

The Early Church's Attitude Toward War

At a time when both the weapons of mass destruction and the ineffectiveness of the just war tradition seem to make Christian participation in war more and more questionable, it becomes increasingly important to examine the witness of the early church.

Modern historical scholarship indicates that for three centuries, all known Christian writings condemned war. In his careful scholarly study entitled *Christian Attitudes toward War and Peace,* Roland Bainton notes that until the early fourth century there is not a single existing Christian writing which supports Christian participation in warfare.[1] Paul Ramsey, the leading contemporary just war theorist, admits that "for almost two centuries of the history of the early church, Christians were universally pacifists."[2] And Ramsey attributes their opposition to war to their theology of the cross: "How could anyone, who knew himself to be classed with transgressors and the enemies of God whom Christ came

"BLESSED ARE
THE PEACEMAKERS
FOR THEY SHALL BE
CALLED THE CHILDREN
OF GOD"

MATTHEW 5 9

to die to save, love his own life and seek to save it more than that of his own enemy or murderer?''[3] . . .

Does this early Christian witness have any relevance for our thermonuclear age? Does nuclear war, perhaps, disclose more clearly than ever before what the early church believed about war? All Christians

agree that the root of war is sin—humanity's idolatrous rebellion against God. Instead of accepting God, Adam and Eve and all their descendants have placed themselves at the center of the universe. This egocentrism has led, since the time of Cain, to a terrible willingness to kill one's neighbor for the sake of one's own interests, values, or nation.

The consequence has been an unending spiral of violence. Clubs gave way to slingshots; longbows to cannon; firebombs to twenty-megaton nuclear warheads. Each new weapon, its creators promised, would preserve the peace. And they usually said it would never be used. But military necessity dictated otherwise. Horrified by each escalation, Christians regularly protested and then reluctantly decided that temporarily, in a fallen world, the new weapons could be used to preserve the peace. But each act of violence led to another. One war always spawned another. Unconditional surrender in World War 1 led to World War 2. Defeating Hitler with the help of Stalin led to two armed superpowers capable of destroying the planet with nuclear weapons. . . .

Why has God allowed us to develop such awful weapons? Undoubtedly because God takes our sinful, stubborn desire to create our own kind of peace and security through violence so seriously that he is willing to let it reach even to nuclear holocaust—unless our desperate predicament forces us to learn that we cannot live without him and that peace and security come not from more deadly weapons but from trust in God. . . .

Disarmament and Difficulties

Christians who work for disarmament must have a realistic view of the formidable barriers which so far have undercut the efforts toward disarmament. This is not to argue that disarmament is impossible. It is simply to recognize that it is one of the most challenging and difficult tasks in the world.

Why has disarmament been so hard to achieve? One reason is human enmity. Even small steps toward disarmament require a willingness to negotiate with one's antagonists. This is very hard to achieve when human inclination to reject love and to follow Cain's murderous ways allows Satan to use us to accomplish his destructive purpose.

Another reason is that disarmament negotiations have been couched in highly technical language. Ordinary people find it hard to understand what is going on when politicians and disarmament negotiators bandy about terms like "strategic asymmetry," "parity," "national technical means" and "window of vulnerability." People around the world come to feel that disarmament is just too technical for the layperson to understand. The reaction is to leave it to the experts. But this means that the only pressure put on the experts is from well-funded lobbies and interest groups that wish to keep the arms race in high gear. Little pressure is felt from the public. This is especially tragic since year after year public opinion polls show that a majority of Americans support disarmament.[4] (Contacts with Soviet citizens also indicate strong support for disarmament and deep yearning for peace, based in no small part on the fact that they lost twenty million people in World War 2.)

In *Nuclear Holocaust & Christian Hope: A Book for Christian Peacemakers*, Ronald J. Sider and Richard K. Taylor tell Christians how to respond to the threat of nuclear war.

Another reason disarmament is difficult is due to the pressure from these interest groups. The military of every country, of course, has an enormous stake in armaments. Military leaders are trained to win. All their past experiences tell them that the side with the most capable armed forces supplied with the biggest, the best and the most weapons is the side that wins. They are suspicious of any suggestion that the size or capability of armies or weapons should be reduced. Furthermore, their jobs and prestige depend on a stable or expanding military budget. It is not surprising, therefore, that generals and admirals in the United States, the Soviet Union, and elsewhere nearly always lobby against disarmament.

Linked with this is the *industrial* side of what President Eisenhower called "the military-industrial complex."[5] This consists of giant corporations which make high profits out of arms sales, unions protecting jobs for workers in defense industries, and university professors who depend on research grants from the Defense Department. They each represent potent and well-financed vested interests which can be counted on to oppose arms reduction. . . .

Politicians are ambivalent about disarmament. They want to represent their constituents' yearning for peace, but they also see no alternative to having weapons to defend their nations against Communist aggression. (Soviet leaders say the same thing about Capitalist imperialism.) Cutting back on weapons may seem a sign of weakness or a loss of national prestige. It may also mean losing defense contracts that promise jobs for the districts they represent.

Another barrier to disarmament is what is technically termed *asymmetry of perception.* This means that, in any potential or actual disarmament talks, each side "perceives" the other differently. There is no objective standard to tell if nations are "even" or if one side is "ahead" of the other in the arms race. Each tends to feel that the *other* is ahead, and that its own side must race harder to keep up. It is extremely difficult to agree on the actual balance of forces between two nations such as the United States and the USSR. Does the fact that we have more nuclear warheads give *us* the lead? Or does the fact that their warheads are bigger and their rockets more powerful give *them* the lead? How do we weigh ambiguous factors like the reliability of each side's allies, differences in geography, access to oceans, and so on? Lacking common values and a common information base, each side tends to see the other as especially threatening and as needing to make the larger disarmament concessions.

Fear also enters in. Neither side trusts the other. Each lives in fear of a disarmament treaty that would give its antagonist a decisive military advantage. Each fears that its competitor may secretly develop new weapons to give it a breakthrough to superiority. Each, therefore, wants to err on the safe side. Each truly believes that things would be better if *its* side were a little ahead.

The problem of "cheating" is another factor complicating the disarmament process. Many politicians and citizens doubt the possibility of verifying whether countries are actually living up to their disarmament agreements. The Soviet Union generally has resisted the idea of disarmament inspectors setting foot on Soviet soil.[6] The problem of on-site inspection has been ameliorated by the development of highly competent means of verification (especially sophisticated photo reconnaissance by satellites) which do not require first-hand observation. Doubt remains on both sides, however, that any verification system can prevent a major violation. . . .

Is Disarmament Possible?

These are staggering obstacles to effective disarmament. Recounting them makes it easy to understand why a dedicated disarmament expert like Alva Myrdal concludes that the six thousand arms control and disarmament negotiations have been little more than a game played by superpowers.[7]

From a Christian point of view, however, these immense obstructions should come as no surprise. The stakes are incredibly high. On the one side is God the Father, setting before us "life and death, blessing and curse," and saying to his children: "Choose life, that you and your descendants may live" (Deut 30:19). On the other side is Satan, the murder, the deceiver, the father of lies, saying to us: Choose death; cling to your weapons; love is foolish; take the way of Cain (cf.1 Jn 3:10). The challenge to Christians is not to be immobilized by the obstacles Satan puts in the path of peace, but to mobilize our deepest prayer, our most intelligent thought, and our most determined action. . . .

The "Nuclear Freeze" Campaign

The most promising current proposal is the call for a mutual "freeze" of nuclear weapons by the United States and the USSR. The call is being put forward by church and peace groups around the world. The proposal is simple and profound at the same time. It says that the way to stop the arms race is to stop. It asks the United States and the Soviet Union to stop all further testing, production, and deployment of nuclear weapons and of the missiles and aircraft designed to carry them. . . .

The freeze idea has enormous advantages as a disarmament proposal. The arms race between the United States and the Soviet Union has proceeded in an upward spiral. We build a missile, and they build a missile to counter it. They increase their military spending; we increase ours. The freeze stops the spiral. It hits the brakes. It gets both sides to stop. It starts to reduce the enormous tensions between the superpowers and therefore reduces the risk of war. . . .

Christians are called to be part of the force which halts the arms race and beckons the nations back from the nuclear abyss. To respond, we must participate in citizen movements that cry for peace so loudly that the world's leaders cannot ignore us. There must be a "new abolitionist movement" which says no to the arms race as forcefully as the old abolitionists said no to slavery. . . .

Nonmilitary Defense

A way out of this dilemma could be found in a defense system which does not rely on military weapons, yet which gives hope of protecting liberties and life. If such a means were available, it could serve as a *substitute,* an alternative, to military defense and war.

The need for an alternative is crucial. People cling to military weapons partly because they believe that they are the only deterrent against aggression. But we believe that there is a method of defense which meets the high call of Jesus to "love your enemies, and pray for those who persecute you" (Mt 5:44). We believe nonmilitary defense is feasible. . . .

Nonmilitary defense might be defined as systematic, organized, active, nonviolent resistance against a power which is regarded as evil, unjust, or contrary to a particular way of life. Its purpose is to protect a nation's freedom and sovereignty and to thwart the goals of an invading enemy. The first and most important characteristic of nonmilitary defense is that it is *active.* It is not a passive, sit-on-your-hands approach, as terms such as *passive resistance* or *nonviolence* might indicate. It is neither weak nor cowardly. It requires both physical and moral courage. This is why the active term *defense* is appropriate.

Yet this is not a defense which uses standard military training and procedures. It is defense as practiced by the entire (or almost entire) population of a country. Hence the expression civilian-based defense (CBD) has become widely used in writings on this subject.[8]

Civilian-based defense encompasses a number of general features. One is that CBD is grounded in *noncooperation.* The population refuses to cooperate with orders, laws, or policies that appear to be evil or unjust. Citizens strike, mount boycotts, refuse to pay taxes. They deny a usurper's sovereignty. They say no to joining his[9] organizations. They accept arrest, exile, or even death rather than assent to tyranny or oppression.

CBD is also *nonviolent.* Rather than replying to the opponent's violence in kind, the defenders suffer under it, seeking simultaneously to limit it, make it ineffective, and end it. In this rejection of violence, CBD is most unlike military defense. But in the expectation of suffering, it is similar. Both CBD and military defense assume that victory demands sacrifice and that people may be injured or die in battle. Both require courage and willingness to take risks. Neither can easily abide what Tom Paine, the American patriot, called "the summer soldier and the sunshine patriot," for both agree with him that "tyranny, like hell, is not easily conquered."

Sometimes another important ingredient is found in CBD—the expression of *good will* toward opponents. We believe that this aspect of CBD is even more crucial than some have thought. . . .

The thought of standing vulnerable before an enemy's nuclear bombs is terrifying. Yet we are vulnerable *now,* even with all our nuclear weapons poised to destroy. If through miscalculation or madness, the Soviet Union launched their ICBMs* at our cities, our most advanced technology could not snatch the missiles from the air and prevent them from decimating our people. *There is no military defense in the nuclear age.* All that we can do is to launch our rockets in retaliation. All that we can do is slit a hundred million enemy throats a few seconds after they have slit ours.

Having nuclear weapons or not having them—both postures involve awesome risk. We face a dark chasm of uncertainty and risk never known before. Obedient faith in Jesus Christ is the only bridge over the chasm. Never in the history of the planet has there been a more desperate need for Jesus's way of costly love for enemies. Jesus taught us to love, not to hate; to heal, not to kill; to pray for our persecutors, not to destroy them. Does he want us now to prepare ourselves massively to kill or massively to love our enemies?

---

*Editor's note: ICBM is an acronym that means intercontinental ballistic missile.

1 Roland H. Bainton, *Christian Attitudes toward War and Peace: A Historical Survey and Critical Re-evaluation* (New York: Abingdon, 1960), p. 53. See also the more recent (1980) book by Hornus, *It Is Not Lawful for Me to Fight,* which has useful and extensive footnotes and a large bibliography.

2 Ramsey, *War and Christian Conscience,* p. xv.

3 Ibid., p. xvi.

4 "In May 1981, a Gallup Poll reported that 72 percent of the respondents favored an agreement with the Soviet Union not to build any more nuclear weapons. Eighty percent favored negotiations with the Soviets to try to reach an agreement." Eugene T. Carroll, "Wanted Alive: Negotiations!" *Coalition Close-Up,* Newsletter of the Coalition for the New Foreign and Military Policy, Fall 1981, p. 3.

5 In his 1961 farewell address, President Eisenhower issued this somber warning: "In the councils of government, we must guard against the acquisition of unwarranted influence, whether sought or unsought, by the military-industrial complex. The potential for the disastrous rise of

misplaced power exists and will persist." Quoted in George Hunsinger, *Idolatry and Prayer: The Arms Race in Theological Perspective* (New York: Riverside Church Disarmament Program, Nov. 1978), p. 7.

[6] It is not true that the USSR has refused all on-site inspection. For example, during negotiations for the Partial Test Ban Treaty, the Soviets expressed willingness to permit three on-site inspections per year on Soviet soil. The Treaty on Peaceful Underground Nuclear Explosions (signed by Moscow and Washington in 1976) provides for on-site inspections, including provisions to assure that observers from the other country can carry out their functions freely and effectively. In general, however, the Soviet stance has been to oppose inspection.

[7] Myrdal, *Game of Disarmament,* p. xviii.

[8] See, for example, Gene Sharp, *Making the Abolition of War a Realistic Goal* (New York: Institute for World Order, 1981), p. 8. Sharp defines CBD as "a defense policy which utilizes prepared civilian struggle—nonviolent action—to preserve the society's freedom, sovereignty, and constitutional system against internal usurpations and external invasions and occupations. The aim is to deter and to defeat such attacks."

[9] We have tried in our own writing to use nonsexist language. One exception, however, is our use of the term *he* or *him* when referring to the invader of a foreign country. We have kept this usage for two reasons. One is that we could not think of any smooth, readable English phrase which would avoid the problem. The other is that, although we realize that women might be involved in the invading force, it is most likely that the majority of the invaders, including the leaders, would be men. The word *he,* therefore, seemed appropriate.

RECOGNIZING AUTHOR'S POINT OF VIEW

This activity may be used as an individualized study guide for students in libraries and resource centers or as a discussion catalyst in small group and classroom discussions.

Many readers are unaware that written material usually expresses an opinion or bias. The skill to read with insight and understanding requires the ability to detect different kinds of bias. Political bias, race bias, sex bias, ethnocentric bias, and religious bias are five basic kinds of opinions expressed in editorials and literature that attempt to persuade. They are briefly defined below.

---

5 Kinds of Editorial Opinion or Bias

SEX BIAS—The expression of dislike for and/or feeling of superiority over a person because of gender or sexual preference

RACE BIAS—The expression of dislike for and/or feeling of superiority over a racial group

ETHNOCENTRIC BIAS—The expression of a belief that one's own group, race, religion, culture, or nation is superior. Ethnocentric persons judge others by their own standards and values.

POLITICAL BIAS—The expression of opinions and attitudes about government-related issues on the local, state, national, or international level

RELIGIOUS BIAS—The expression of a religious belief or attitude

---

Guidelines

1. Locate three examples of political opinion or bias in the readings from chapter two.

2. Locate five sentences that provide examples of any kind of editorial opinion or bias from the readings in chapter two.

3. Write down each of the above sentences and determine what kind of bias each sentence represents. Is it *sex bias, race bias, ethnocentric bias, political bias,* or *religious bias?*

4. Make up one sentence statements that would be an example of each of the following: *sex bias, race bias, ethnocentric bias, political bias, and religious bias.*

5. See if you can locate five sentences that are factual statements from the readings in chapter two.

Summarize author's point of view in one sentence for each of the following opinions:

Reading 9 _____

_____

Reading 10 _____

_____

Reading 11 _____

_____

Reading 12 _____

_____

Reading 13 _____

_____

Reading 14 _____

_____

CHAPTER 3

THE TELEVANGELISTS

INTRODUCTION

Chapter three examines the issue of television preachers and the electronic church and focuses on two particular philosophical issues, as explained below.

► Readings 15 and 16 refer to the PTL sex scandal, which occurred in 1987 when televangelist Jimmy Swaggart* exposed fellow televangelist and PTL Television Network founder Jim Bakker's affair with a former church secretary. Subsequent investigation revealed Bakker's payment of "hush money," the Bakkers' lavish lifestyle, and misuse of PTL funds. Although the PTL incident is in the past, it brought an important issue to the surface: Are television ministries open and accountable? This question remains timeless.

► Readings 17 and 18 discuss televangelist Pat Robertson and his involvement in politics. Once again, this highly specific example allows us to examine the age-old, philosophical questions regarding religion and politics.

---

*On February 21, 1988, Jimmy Swaggart, who reportedly was photographed with a prostitute, said he would step out of the pulpit until church officials complete an investigation, reportedly for allegations of sexual misconduct.

THE TELEVANGELISTS

THE GOSPEL OF JESUS CHRIST

Jerry Falwell

The Reverend Jerry Falwell is the founder of the Thomas Road Baptist Church, "The Old-Time Gospel Hour," Liberty University, and the Moral Majority.

Falwell wrote the following column shortly after the PTL sex scandal. The column appeared in Liberty Report, *a publication of Falwell's Liberty Federation.*

Points to Consider:

1. Why did Falwell write this column?
2. Does Falwell live in an extravagant manner? Are Falwell's ministries open and accountable? Provide examples to support your answers.
3. Summarize the ways in which Falwell's ministries preach the Gospel of Jesus Christ.
4. Define the term "health-and-wealth" theology.

Jerry Falwell, "Christian Media Ministries in Trouble," *Liberty Report,* May 1987, pp. 2, 24-25.

It is very important that all Christian ministries, from local churches to the largest electronic ministries, develop a commitment to openness and accountability.

The Bible says that "we should be ready always to give an answer to every man. . ."

You have probably been asked some hard questions lately because others know you are Jerry Falwell's friend. You may be having some questions of your own. I hope this column will help you answer those questions.

The Assault on Media Ministries

It is doubtful that the cause of Jesus Christ has ever suffered a greater tragedy than during the past several weeks.

The credibility of every Bible-believing pastor, evangelist, and church in America has been greatly damaged.

No doubt you have read about:

(1) the sex scandal at PTL,
(2) the payment of "hush money,"
(3) the alleged multi-million dollar lifestyles of some ministers,
(4) the lack of audited financial statements and full disclosure of financial dealings by some ministries, and
(5) the questionable fund-raising tactics employed by some, etc., etc.

Every newspaper in America has carried these very sad stories in their headlines recently. All the major television networks have made this the top story. *And the assault is not over yet.*

While only a very few persons are guilty of these kinds of misconduct, enemies and critics of Christian television have used this opportunity to indict every pastor who preaches the gospel over the media. The battle is on to force Christian ministries off the air.

They would like to convince the American public that *all* evangelical and fundamentalist Christian ministries on television and radio are dishonest and unworthy of the financial support of Christian people.

Fewer Contributions

And I must assume that they have succeeded at this somewhat. *Many of our friends and supporters have been strangely silent in the last several weeks.* We estimate that our losses at the Old Time Gospel Hour now exceed $2 million from anticipated contributions that did not materialize. And although we have received very few critical letters from our friends, a large number of them have not contributed in recent days.

115

As a result, *Old Time Gospel Hour, Liberty University, the Liberty Godparent Ministry, and Liberty Federation are suffering financially. I can understand this reluctance to give.*

I have talked with many of the Christian broadcasters in America. They are also hurting. There is a deep concern that even local churches are being penalized. There is a general fear and distrust in the hearts and minds of many American people today because of sinful deeds committed by a few persons who name the name of Christ.

Maybe many of our friends and supporters are wondering about me. Maybe they are asking themselves—Is Jerry Falwell honest? Is he playing games?

And for that reason, I am writing this column.

Jerry Falwell: Servant of God

I believe it is my duty to attempt to clear up any doubts or questions people may have and help them answer the questions critics may direct their way.

For 31 years, I have been pastor of the Thomas Road Baptist Church in Lynchburg, Virginia. God allowed me to start this congregation in 1956 with 35 charter members. We have 22,000 members today. In our city of Lynchburg and surrounding counties, there is a population of approximately 110,000. Obviously, this means a significant percentage of all the residents of this area belong to Thomas Road Baptist Church.

I am accountable, on a daily basis, to these 22,000 church members. I am also responsible to the deacon board of Thomas Road Baptist Church.

JERRY FALWELL

Since I have spent all 53 years of my life in this little town, virtually everyone knows me by name and by face. The Bible requires that the servant of God be "blameless" and "above reproach"—*and this kind of accountability is scriptural.*

I feel that I am also accountable to the public as far as our finances are concerned.

Therefore, the annual financial statements of Old Time Gospel Hour, Thomas Road Baptist Church, Liberty University, and all related ministries are made available upon request to all donors—and have been for years.

Coopers and Lybrand, one of the top ten auditing firms in America, are our independent auditors.

No Exorbitant Salaries

I also want to report that Jerry Falwell earns a reasonable salary from Thomas Road Baptist Church and Old Time Gospel Hour. Furthermore, we pay no exorbitant salaries to any of our 2,000 staff people. They would say a hearty *Amen* to this.

The pastors and staff members of this ministry believe that God has called them to the work they are doing here. They fully understand that they could probably earn a great deal more money working for enterprises in the secular marketplace.

I am often given honoraria for speaking engagements. As an author, I earn advances and royalties from books I write. And because I am in a high profile position, these fees and royalties are often more than I deserve.

My wife and I try to faithfully share with the Lord's work the funds that He places in our hands. *I will not be ashamed to stand before the Lord with our stewardship record.*

No Ostentatious Living

As for the house in which we live, a board member of the Old Time Gospel Hour personally purchased our home in 1980 for $160,000. He then donated the home to the Thomas Road Baptist Church and Old Time Gospel Hour as a parsonage.

The home was built in 1834. And my wife and I have enjoyed renovating and improving this beautiful old colonial home during the past seven years.

The donor requested that the ministry one day consider giving the homeplace to Macel and me. When the ministry decided to do this, Macel and I refused. Instead, we elected to buy the home from the ministry at the original purchase price. *We are making payments on our home right now.*

I do not own a Rolls Royce or drive a luxury automobile.

I drive a 4-wheel drive GMC suburbantype truck. I was born on a farm in Campbell County, Virginia in 1933. And although they have gotten this boy out of the farm—they have not gotten the farm out of me.

I still prefer a truck over a car. I do not waste money. Nor do the Falwells live in an ostentatious way.

An Open and Accountable Ministry

Not one penny ever contributed to the Old Time Gospel Hour or any of our ministries has ever gone into my pocket, or into the pockets of the pastors or Christian workers who labor in this ministry.

I understand the doubts and fears that have been raised in the minds of good American people as a result of the sordid events of the past few weeks.

And that is why I want to be as open and honest as I possibly can about our ministry here. I call upon all Christian leaders to go the extra mile in this area of accountability and openness. I sincerely believe the vast majority of pastors and evangelists are honest and sincere. We must not allow the misconduct of a handful to cripple the overall cause of Christ.

We are presently making available an unabridged copy of the Old Time Gospel Hour Ministry and Financial Report to every donor to our ministries.

I think most persons would be excited to learn all that is going on here in Lynchburg and around the world.

For example, it has now been *31 years* that we have been *preaching the Gospel of Jesus Christ* to multiplied millions of souls through the Old Time Gospel Hour television and radio program . . .

. . . and there are now *7,500* bright young men and women who are training to become *champions for Christ* on our 4,700 acre campus of Liberty University . . .

. . . God has allowed us to *plant and assume the pastorate of* over *900 churches* nationwide with our graduates and send missionaries into many different nations around the world. Right now, we support missionaries in 66 nations . . .

. . . the Liberty Godparent Home continues to offer hope and salvation to thousands of pregnant teenage girls who have contacted us for help, seeking an alternative to abortion . . .

. . . and God has allowed us to bring joy to many childless Christian couples through our adoption agency . . .

. . . every year we are able to send trained young people into the inner cities of America's metropolitan areas—areas like New York, Philadelphia, Los Angeles, Detroit, Washington, and others where the power of the gospel is desperately needed . . .

. . . exposure teams from the Liberty University also go into many different parts of Europe, South America, Africa, and other parts of the world, witnessing for Jesus Christ . . .

. . . our ministry to senior saints, children, and young people touches literally hundreds of thousands of lives. Over 3,000 junior and senior high school young people recently participated in an evangelistic campaign at Thomas Road Baptist Church where 300 accepted Christ as their personal Savior. . .

. . .our Elim Home for Alcoholics has been offering deliverance from drunkenness to literally hundreds of alcoholic men during the past 29 years. They all participate in this ministry without cost. . .

. . .as far as I know, God has given us the largest ministry to the deaf in the world. . .

. . .the Fundamentalist Journal magazine and our newspaper, the *Liberty Report,* minister to over 2 million persons monthly. . .

. . .the large Counseling Center on Liberty Mountain reaches out to thousands of hurting people year after year. . .

. . .our missions to the military is very effective. And our prison ministry is touching hundreds of thousands of hardened criminals, with the Gospel of Jesus Christ.

We want our donors to be confident and sure that we are indeed who we say we are—that we are doing exactly what we claim to be doing.

We want them to know that we are honest and above-board, and that their contributions are used exactly as designated.

Of course, I am prejudiced, but I believe contributions to the Old Time Gospel Hour, Liberty University, the Liberty Godparent Home and the other ministries in Lynchburg may be the best investment of God's money in the world today—and I also think a personal visit to Lynchburg, Virginia would convince anyone of the accuracy of this claim.

Now, with all these self-serving statements aside, it is very important that all Christian ministries, from local churches to the largest electronic ministries, develop a commitment to openness and accountability. Both the Scriptures and the hour demand it.

God Must Purge His Church

It is also important that we pray for revival in America. Revival does not come without genuine repentance. Materialism and the new "health-and-wealth" theology are corrupting Christianity. We must repudiate these damnable heresies. We must likewise call America's Christian leaders to account for immoral conduct. We must condemn the greedy and selfish financial dealings of those who pretend to be pastors and evangelists. Judgment must begin at the house of God.

Clearly, God must purge His church before revival can come. At this moment, there is a sovereign move of Almighty God against all sin and degradation that is being performed in the name of God. In my opinion, this move will not stop until God has finished his purifying work.

THE TELEVANGELISTS

THE GOSPEL
OF WEALTH AND POWER

Jim Wallis

Jim Wallis is the editor of Sojourners *magazine, an independent Christian monthly. He is also a member of the Sojourners Community in Washington, D.C. and is the author of numerous books and articles on religion and peace and justice issues.*

Wallis wrote the following column in Sojourners *shortly after the PTL sex scandal.*

Points to Consider:

1. Examine the Bible verse at the beginning of the reading (Galatians 5:19-23). Why do you think the author chose to use this particular verse?
2. Compare and contrast Jesus and the early Christians with today's TV preachers.
3. Explain how money and power have affected TV evangelism.
4. Why did it take a highly publicized scandal to break open the world of the televangelists?

Jim Wallis, "The Real Scandal," *Sojourners,* June 1987, pp. 4-5. Reprinted with permission from *Sojourners,* Box 29272, Washington, D.C. 20017.

Now the works of the flesh are plain: immorality, impurity, licentiousness, idolatry, sorcery, enmity, strife, jealousy, anger, selfishness, dissension, factions, envy, drunkenness, carousing, and the like. . . . But the fruit of the Spirit is love, joy, peace, patience, kindness, goodness, faithfulness, gentleness, self-control; against such there is no law.

Galatians 5:19-23

Soap-Like Scandal

The high and unholy public drama being played out by the nation's leading television evangelists should put to rest any lingering fear that the Christian media might not be as entertaining as the real thing. "Days of Our Lives," "General Hospital," and "The Young and the Restless" have all taken a back seat to the emerging soap-like scandal that has embroiled and embattled many of the most celebrated TV preachers. Overwhelmed, and now overcome, by the traditional temptations of money, sex, and power, the media ministers-turned-media moguls have displayed, before the eyes of the nation, behavior that is at the same time absurd, disgusting, and just plain tasteless.

"We're ashamed, we're embarrassed, we're humiliated, and we're dismayed about all these problems surfacing in the media across the nation," lamented Rev. G. Raymond Carlson, who heads the pentecostal Assemblies of God denomination, in which two of the principal combatants in the present crisis, Jim Bakker and Jimmy Swaggart, are ordained ministers. Carlson speaks for many in the pentecostal and fundamentalist Christian communities, from which the TV evangelists draw most of their viewers, but also for the wider evangelical movement and even the broader church.

Painful Disillusionment

Tales of adultery, hush money, hostile takeovers, power plays, ego clashes, financial empires, and personal fortunes have grabbed headlines across the nation while providing fresh, new material for Johnny Carson's smirking monologues and the yuppie cynicism of David Letterman and "Saturday Night Live." As church people are embarrassed or defensive, religious hypocrisy is again served up to an already skeptical public as further justification for unbelief. Even worse is the painful disillusionment of millions of faithful Christian viewers and supporters—ordinary, hardworking, decent, and devout people—whose lives, unlike their TV preacher heroes, would not qualify for "Lifestyles of the Rich and Famous."

122

One wants to believe that these TV ministers began with genuine sincerity and ardent faith in earlier and more innocent days. But, as in all things, the dangers of success can so easily corrupt fledgling hopes and dreams. An incident of sexual misconduct and a resulting cover-up catalyzed a power struggle between rival evangelists competing for high stakes—prestige, ratings, and most of all, money—in a very lucrative but increasingly crowded religious media market.

Sexual Morality

But one must also ask why it took a highly publicized, scintillating, and sordid scandal to finally break open the world of the televangelists and begin to focus some hard questions on the media empires these electronic men of the cloth have created. An obvious answer is that the scandal was about sex, a constant preoccupation of the media, popular culture, and religion.

But, from a biblical perspective, aren't the moral issues of money and power at least as important as sexual morality? Those questions regarding the empires and activities of the TV preachers have been growing in significance for some time now. Unfortunately for them and for all of us, these were questions that most others in the wider church chose to ignore.

From the view of Christian ethics, sex is indeed important. The integrity of our sexual values, relationships, and morality is vitally connected to a whole, healthy, and truly human life. The biblical values of commitment, faithfulness, and fidelity cannot be stressed enough in these sexually confused and troubled times. But that said, it must also be said that sexual morality isn't the only biblical morality. Beneath the present furor over a televangelist's sexual conduct, are there not also theological, spiritual, and political transgressions that are themselves great scandals to the gospel?

123

Cartoon by David Seavey. Copyright 1987, *USA Today.* Reprinted with permission.

"Follow the Money"

At a crucial juncture in the Watergate investigations, the famous source "Deep Throat" gave some advice to *Washington Post* reporter Bob Woodward: "Follow the money." Unfortunately, that is good advice in getting to the bottom of any scandal, including this one. In TV evangelism, money has become the means, the method, and the measure of success.

The few exceptions, such as Billy Graham, are so different from the TV preachers who regularly fill the airwaves that the clear comparison helps to make the point. The sums of money have become enormous in the religious media, the projects and "ministries" endless, the fund-raising constant and fiercely competitive. The lifestyles of the televangelists bear the stamps of celebrity status more than the marks of sacrificial discipleship.

Jesus had no place to lay his head, and the early Christians shared all they had with the poor. In stark and glittering contrast are the mansions, cars, clothes, and entourages of these modern media disciples—all of which have been taken to ridiculous and embarrassing extremes in "Christian" fashion shows, shopping malls, resort hotels, and theme parks complete with religious water slides for the kids.

The opulent extravagances of the TV evangelists in a world where most of God's children are hungry and poor is the real scandal here. Money, of course, affects and radically alters theology. The result and rationale of such crass materialism is the prosperity gospel of wealth and health, created and boldly proclaimed by many of the TV preachers. This self-serving message had led to a moral bankruptcy far more serious than the economic bankruptcy they so fear. Loudly proclaimed and very token offerings to "the poor" simply compound the offense.

Dubious Fundraising

The sad picture of an aging evangelist, holed up in his prayer tower, threatening that God would "take me home" if enough money didn't come in is different only in degree but not in kind from the high-pressure, money-raising tactics of his colleagues. Fund-raising practices universally recognized as unethical, such as the "bait and switch" method—raising money ostensibly for one thing (often starving children) but using the funds for something else (usually general operating expenses)—have become the norm for many of the TV evangelists.

Even when proof of such dubious practices has become available to other evangelical leaders and institutions, little if anything has been said or done. New concern for financial disclosure and accountability among religious organizations is a welcome sign. Time will tell how much real change occurs.

Power and Politics

After money and sex, power is the other issue this current conflict raises. But rather than just lament the lack of love the preachers have shown each other in their transparent ego clashes, we must look more deeply at the spiritual wisdom of such power bases and power brokering in the first place.

Each successful evangelist has established his own little, but expanding, empire that may include television studios, stations, and even networks; Bible schools and universities; political organizations; and even luxury hotels and amusement parks. Each conglomerate is run like a personal fiefdom for the evangelist, who is accountable to no one.

That power, counted by numbers of viewers, members, donors, students, and most of all, dollars, has been projected onto the national political stage since the presidential election of 1980. Christian faith certainly has political implications, and Christians have a right, and even a responsibility, to help shape the direction of their nation. But are the political brokering, back-room deals, and the eager embracing of political power enthusiastically practiced by the TV preachers characteristic of a biblical approach?

Isn't a more independent, critical, and prophetic role more in keeping with the scriptural tradition? And isn't the Religious Right's equation of conservative, capitalist, Republican politics with the kingdom of God as wrong as those religionists who conform to the liberal Left? And, finally, isn't the strident American nationalism preached by mostly rich white men a dangerous substitute for the reconciling work of Christ, which knows no national boundaries and overcomes the divisions of race, class, and sex?

Very partisan political power is no fit replacement for the power of God upon which gospel preachers must finally rely. The intimacy the televangelists have enjoyed with the present administration and their complicity with the political Far Right have been morally compromising and undermining of a truly independent Christian political witness.

Demand Accountability

The scandal and embarrassment of the television evangelists did not begin with the present crisis. Its roots are deeper, the issues broader, and the transgressions go farther back. Why weren't the churches, the evangelical community in particular, and the evangelical establishment most particularly, raising the tough questions earlier, subjecting the burgeoning TV empires to biblical criteria, theological scrutiny, and spiritual wisdom? Why was no accountability demanded earlier? (New efforts to do just that, especially in the area of evangelical fund raising, are laudable but late.)

The people and institutions with the clearest responsibility for seeking accountability from the TV preachers, for the most part, failed to act. Those who should have said and done more, and didn't, now must share responsibility for the damage of the now revealed scandals. Why didn't things get said and done earlier? Because most of us won't argue with success, wealth, and power, not even in the church. When will we learn?

THE TELEVANGELISTS

PAT ROBERTSON: SPIRITUAL LEADER

Bob G. Slosser

Bob G. Slosser is the co-author of Pat Robertson's book, The Secret Kingdom. *He graduated from the University of Maine and is the author of several books. He has also served as assistant national editor of* The New York Times, *editor of* The National Courier, *and executive vice-president of The Christian Broadcasting Network, Inc.*

Points to Consider:

1. Compare Pat Robertson's understanding of the Constitution to the Founding Fathers' original intent.
2. According to the author, what have been the outcomes of humanistic philosophy? Why does the author believe Pat Robertson can tackle these problems?
3. Why does the author believe Pat Robertson would be a strong leader?
4. Summarize why the author believes Pat Robertson should be the President.

Bob G. Slosser, "Why I Believe the Right Should be for Pat Robertson," *Conservative Digest,* October 1987, pp. 61, 63, 65-66. Reprinted with permission of *Conservative Digest.*

His close reading of the United States and world history buttresses Pat Robertson's compelling concern about the morality, the ethics, the goodness of the American people.

I met Pat Robertson one bright New England spring morning in 1967. We were breakfast guests of mutual friends in Weston, Massachusetts, a prosperous suburb of Boston. Pat was on one of many trips to Boston that ultimately led to a Christian Broadcasting Network (CBN) television outlet there.

As a newsman and a new Christian, I was quickly struck by two things: Robertson was obviously a man of faith, a devout man if you will, and he was a man of action in a hard-driving, rough-and-tough world. His youthful vigor, smiling good looks of John F. Kennedy, and sincerity of mission were not at all the characteristics that one like myself had come to expect from "religious" people. This was not a man destined for an obscure life in the pulpit or pew. His vision was wider than that.

Moving steadily from liberalism to conservatism over the next twenty years, I watched the development of Robertson—like most Virginians a Democrat in those early years—as a national thinker and leader, finding myself often startled by the breadth and depth of that development.

Pat is rare among leaders today because of his grasp of the essentials of America. In a 25-year news career, I had a good seat from which to watch our times unfold. And, by the way, that's the sum of the advantages of a newsman today—a better seat, not greater intelligence, not greater wisdom, not greater accuracy. And from that choice seat I watched leaders come and go across the national scene. I watched political leaders, social leaders, business leaders, media leaders. Yes, I watched as leaders dwindled and faded into virtual nothingness. Their weakness had to do with the essentials of America. They, with a handful of exceptions, had lost touch with this land and its people.

As a conservative, I find that critically important. We need leadership in every sector that understands this country and the way it works. This calls for wisdom and knowledge of the past and of the present. And that brings us to the Constitution of the United States.

Our Constitution

As for the past, our leaders must understand the foundation of the nation—the Constitution, which set us in motion and keeps us in motion as one nation under God, a nation of laws that refuses to shift with the whims and prejudices of erratic men. I remember a conversation with Robertson and a group of knowledgeable political supporters on the patio of his home in Virginia Beach. The question was simple: "As a man of God, how would you govern if elected?" The reply was also simple: "I would *govern* by the Constitution and *lead* by example."

WHY PAT ROBERTSON WANTS TO BE PRESIDENT

Pat is considering a run for the presidency because the history of his entire adult professional life inclines him to think in terms of service.

Pat also believes God is calling him into public life, and he is earnestly seeking the Lord's instruction on the matter.

Hundreds of thousands of people see Pat as a thoughtful, articulate, and moral champion for traditional American and family values. These people throughout the nation are encouraging Pat to give serious consideration to seeking the presidency.

The combination of their encouragement, Pat's sense of obligation to serve, and an inner peace in his life that would indicate this is God's will, have prompted him to consider running for this political office.

The Christian Broadcasting Network, 1987

Through study as a law student at Yale and years of related work, Robertson stands foursquare on the Constitution and has been strong in his denunciations of those who have tampered with it in the last 30 years from the Supreme Court bench or anywhere else. And he knows full well that as a man of religious belief there is no conflict between his faith and the Constitution. The founders had no conflict, and neither does he. The founders were adamant against the establishment of any national religion or church. So is Robertson. The founders were adamant against any law or interpretation that would prevent an individual from exercising his religious faith. So is Robertson.

Also springing from his commitment to the Constitution is Pat Robertson's apparent understanding that a central obligation of the federal government is to guarantee the security of the United States. It must have defensive forces to stand against the renegade nations of the world. America must be able to defend herself—quickly—if she, her citizens, and the citizens of other like-minded nations of the world are to remain free. Such an understanding is not in conflict with that of men and women of religious conviction.

As a conservative who watched the deterioration of our defensive ability in the Seventies, I find this terribly important. Our nation has provided more freedom than any in history, and our ability to defend ourselves and others has been central to that fact. Robertson is sound on defense.

Pat Robertson, founder of the Christian Broadcasting Network.

Good Character

His close reading of the United States and world history buttresses Pat Robertson's compelling concern about the morality, the ethics, the goodness of the American people. Of course, many leaders present a loose, lip-service concern for those matters that touch the character of our nation. They scream over symptoms, but give very little attention to the core of the problem, which is a blindness to the fact that there is right and there is wrong, there is good and there is bad, there is truth and there is falsehood.

As a conservative, I want leaders who perceive that for years many of America's intellectuals have tried to take our country down a disastrous path. These people have tried to instill in us a humanistic philosophy that panders to self-concern, greed, and materialism. It is a philosophy that says grab everything you can get, don't be concerned about anyone but yourself, don't worry about who's responsible. It is a philosophy that leads to unrestrained abortion, pornography in every form, every kind of crime imaginable, total madness in the use of alcohol and drugs, disastrous deterioration of the family, unwillingness to fight to preserve the national good. It is a philosophy that leads to relativism, selfishness, weakness, corruption, and ultimately to national collapse.

Pat Robertson seems to recognize the key ingredients in this hedonistic nightmare. He is the only one among the candidates and prospective candidates who appears to understand that these questions of national and individual morality eventually touch every issue. Why are the others afraid of these issues? Judgment, of course, does not belong to me, but it does seem that the question of character should be raised.

Can Robertson be the only one who sees into the core of the threat to the national fiber? Is he the only one who recognizes that grass-roots America does not want to go this way? Is he the only one to see the widening division between those who have governed and those who have been governed for much of the last 25 years? If so, all the more reason to choose Pat Robertson.

Leadership

Earlier I spoke of the need for leaders with knowledge of the past and of the present. As a conservative, I want a strong leader who wants a strong nation, but not a strong centralized government. The path to strength for this nation is not one that calls for the federal government to do everything—and that takes us back to the constitutional issue again. Some matters belong properly with an efficient, honest, and well-balanced government. But those matters are far fewer than our leaders have thought in much of the final two-thirds of this century.

We need wisdom and restraint in leadership, not coercion. True leadership is just that: leadership. As Pat Robertson has said, it comes through the Constitution and through example. It must be articulate, sincere, and persevering.

I've had numerous national newsmen ask me in the last two years my view of the single quality that makes Robertson deserving of the Presidency. The answer has been easy, despite the fact that it obviously sounds like political puffery: He can lead.

Pat Robertson has been leading most of his life, in varying arenas— as a prep schoolboy, as the son of a U.S. Senator, as a Phi Beta Kappa student at Washington and Lee, as a Marine officer, as a law student at Yale, as a seminary student in New York, as a minister in a Brooklyn ghetto, as the founder of a television network, as the founder of a graduate university, as the host of a major daily TV program reaching 43 nations, as the developer of an international philanthropic outreach, as the operator of a significant television station in the Middle East, as a best-selling author, as the founder of a religious-liberty legal unit to counter the rampages of the American Civil Liberties Union (A.C.L.U.), and as a husband and father of four children making notable accomplishments in several areas.

Again, I've told newsmen that Robertson's leadership springs from several facts: He is very bright, he is well educated, he is a man of extraordinary faith in God, he does many things well. And, most important in our day, he is a magnificent communicator. Because of my work as an observer of some quite good communicators, both in and out of politics, I usually tell inquiring newsmen, "You haven't seen anything yet."

Communications skills can be used for many purposes—some good, some not so good. That's why it's terribly important that they be founded on something deeper than skill. Moral character, for example.

A Winning Combination

Over the last 25 years Pat Robertson has reached a lot of Americans. They've seen him on television daily and they've seen him in person on every kind of occasion—from church services to educational meetings to political rallies. He is the only one among those conservatives gazing fondly at the Presidency who has genuine grass-roots support. Furthermore, he has a grass-roots organization that has already shown its effectiveness in the states of Michigan and South Carolina.

In other words, he has communicated for years with the grass-roots people—the Americans—and he continues to do so. When they listen, they like him.

And that translates into a fact that the doubting Thomases must hear: He can win. That's important.

He will do well in Iowa. He will do well in New Hampshire. He will do well in the big Southern event. Then look out. The numbers are there.

As a conservative who arrived at my views the hard way—through failed liberalism and by discarding wishy-washy neutrality—I believe my fellow conservatives need to do what increasing numbers of good, persevering Americans are doing: Listen to what Pat Robertson is saying, listen to him on the issues. He's consistent, he's thorough, he's appealing, and he can win.

Ronald Reagan has done many things right in the last seven years. He has restored a love of country to many parts of the land. He has made it respectable to be a patriot. He has fought against big government and big spending in spite of the congressional roadblocks that have tripped him. He has made strong strides toward a proper national defense.

But he's faltered at some points, mostly having to do with questionable selection of people around him, who failed to stand firm on Reagan ground. Those questionable choices often severed the great communicator's ties to his natural grass-roots constituency. I am confident Pat Robertson will not make those mistakes.

18 THE TELEVANGELISTS

PAT ROBERTSON: POLITICAL EXTREMIST

People for the American Way

People for the American Way is a non-partisan constitutional liberties organization that was founded in 1980. Since then, "it has monitored and countered the Religious Right's religious intolerance and effort to use religion to disguise a partisan, extreme right-wing agenda."

Points to Consider:

1. Analyze Pat Robertson's "pipeline" to God.
2. Describe Pat Robertson's stand on separation of church and state.
3. How do Pat Robertson's views on the Constitution contrast with American tradition?
4. Summarize Pat Robertson's beliefs with regard to education and women's rights.

Jim Castelli, *Pat Robertson: Extremist* (Washington, D.C.: People for the American Way, 1986).

Robertson is, very simply, an extremist whose views place him well outside the mainstream of both the Republican Party and the nation.

Introduction

The New Republic magazine has dubbed presidential hopeful Pat Robertson the "Teflon Telepreacher" because criticism has not stuck to him. Robertson has indeed been lucky—he's had visibility, but not exposure. After Robertson's strong showing in early Michigan caucuses to choose delegates for the 1988 Republican Convention, media coverage has moved quickly to the "horse race" stage, focusing on Robertson's strength and potential impact on the choice of the 1988 Republican presidential nominee.

Robertson has also benefitted from association with others in the public arena: former President Jimmy Carter was a born-again Christian; Jesse Jackson is a Baptist minister; President Reagan is a conservative. Finally, Robertson's personal manner—smooth, polished, smiling, reassuring—is not threatening.

All of these factors have combined to obscure the fact that Pat Robertson is, very simply, an extremist whose views place him well outside the mainstream of both the Republican Party and the nation. At one level, Robertson offers the extremism of the Religious Right, with its claims of a divinely mandated political agenda. At another level, Robertson offers views long associated with secular right-wing extremists. . . .

Pat's Pipeline to God

For almost a quarter of a century, Robertson has claimed to receive detailed answers from God to problems in his professional life.

The pages of Robertson's first book, *Shout It From the Rooftops* (1972) are full of references to God's involvement in the early days of Robertson's broadcasting career. Robertson told the owner of a small TV station he wanted to buy, "God has sent me here to buy your television station. . . .God's figure is $37,000, and the station has to be free from all debts and encumbrances.". . .

In his book *Beyond Reason: How Miracles Can Change Your Life* (1984), a "how-to" book about working miracles, Robertson, who claims to be a faith-healer, says that during the 1960s, God turned a hurricane away from Virginia Beach to spare the CBN tower and has kept the area free of hurricanes ever since: "As I prayed out loud. . .faith rose within me, and with authority in my voice, I found myself speaking to a giant, killer hurricane about one hundred miles away in the Atlantic Ocean. Specifically, I commanded that storm, in the name of Jesus, to stop its forward movement and to head back where it had come from." Robertson says the hurricane stopped in its tracks at the precise time he had commanded it to stop and later made a 180-degree turn.

"Skeptics may offer other explanations for these events. But I know it was God's power that spared this region and also our CBN's tower.". . .

History shows that Americans like their presidents to pray. That attitude does not reflect mere piety; it has a very practical dimension as well. Presidents who pray and feel awed by God's power presumably have a strong sense of humility and that, convenient denials aside, he sees no difference between God's will and his own personal ambitions.

Robertson's Two Views of Church-State Separation

The question of whether or not Pat Robertson has a personal pipeline to God is not the only issue...Robertson tells mainstream media outlets that he supports the separation of church and state; but when he talks to his "700 Club" audience or conservative outlets, he takes a much different line, attacking the separation of church and state as an "atheistic communist" idea. . . .

Robertson has repeatedly argued that the U.S. Constitution says nothing about the separation of church and state but that the phrase appears in the Soviet Constitution. He claims that after the Soviet Constitution was written, a new doctrine came into being in 1920 with the creation of the American Civil Liberties Union; that doctrine, he said, was designed to remove religion from American life and to bring U.S. policy in line with that of the Soviet Union. ("700 Club," Sept. 30, 1981). . . .

Robertson has, on a number of occasions, described government as an arm of religion and argued for certain public policies not on the basis of their merits, but on the basis that he finds them in the Bible. . . .

► Robertson says the only way to reduce the national budget deficit is to follow biblical guidance: "The debt is what the problem is. . .and every 50 years, God said 'Let's declare a Year of Jubilee, cancel all the debts and get on with it.' But we don't follow God's way and so we get caught on this hook again." ("700 Club," May 28, 1982); "God's way is every 50 years to have a Jubilee and cancel

136

Cartoon by William Sanders. Reprinted with special permission of NAS, Inc.

all the debts. . .that is the only way to solve the recession and national debt." ("700 Club," July 15, 1982). . . .

▶ Robertson said he supports the death penalty because "The judicial execution of a rebel against society has never been forbidden by the Bible." (*USA Today,* June 27, 1986). . . .

▶ Robertson told *Time* magazine "The prophet Isaiah says we are supposed to lift the yoke of oppression. . . . Pacifism is not biblical. We have to realize that we are dealing with a malevolent power that over the last four decades has resulted in the death of over 250 million human beings. There has never been a force in the history of the world that has been as vicious, as malevolent, and at its core, atheistic and desirous of destroying the liberties of people. I think that if we have the opportunity to assist these wars of liberation, as in Afghanistan or Nicaragua or Angola, we should do that. We have no obligation to assist the enemies of the U.S. or the enemies of the Lord or the enemies of freedom." (Feb. 17, 1986). . . .

It is clear that Robertson pays lip service to "the separation of church and state" while simultaneously trying to smear the concept as a communistic notion. It is also clear that he finds justifications for specific public policy options in the Bible in a manner that is clearly contrary to the traditional American concept of church-state separation because it would form public policy on the basis of sectarian doctrine.

Armageddon Theology

Robertson's reference in a *Time* interview to biblical prophecies about the Middle East stem from his belief in "Armageddon Theology," a form of fundamentalism which holds that the Bible offers a detailed prophetic description of events—including war in the Middle East—leading to the Second Coming of Christ and the end of the world. . . .

Robertson has discussed Armageddon Theology in detail on "The 700 Club." On one show, Ben Kinchlow* asked "Does the Bible specifically tell us what is going to happen in the future?" Robertson replied, "It sure does, Ben. . .it specifically, clearly, unequivocally (says). . .that Russia and other countries will enter into war and God will destroy Russia through earthquakes, volcanoes, etc." (Dec. 3, 1981). After the Israeli invasion of Lebanon in 1982, Robertson predicted a Soviet-led invasion of Israel that could put the world "in flames" by the end of the year and lead to the Second Coming by the year 2000. (*Newsweek,* July 5, 1982). On May 20, 1982, Robertson said "The Bible says that. . .the Soviet Union is going to make a move against this little nation known as Israel. And that's got to happen because it is very clear cut in the Bible in the last days; and along with the Soviet Union there is going to be Iran, there is going to be Ethiopia, possibly Libya, some East German forces which are now in South Yemen, this is going to happen. . .there is going to be a move by the Soviet Union into the Middle East.". . .

Armageddon Theology clearly has political implications. The greatest danger it presents is a disdain for peace, particularly in the Middle East. Robertson was particularly pessimistic about the prospects for peace in the wake of the Israeli invasion of Lebanon. . . .

Robertson's disdain for peace extends to the Soviet Union, which, as an "atheistic, humanistic" empire is clearly linked to the power of Satan in his worldview. . . .

---

*Editor's note: Ben Kinchlow is the former co-host of "The 700 Club." He resigned on Jan. 26, 1988, saying he was "going home to seek the Lord." Kinchlow joined "The 700 Club" in 1975.

The Law According To Pat Robertson

One of Pat Robertson's ancestors signed the Declaration of Independence, and, by a strange brand of logic, Robertson believes this makes him an expert on the U.S. Constitution. He spends at least as much time discussing the Constitution as he does any other single issue. But Robertson's views of the Constitution, the federal courts and the rule of law in general are at odds with the American tradition and represent a major example of the merging of the extremism of his theopolitical views and the extremism of secular right-wing movements....

For example, he once declared, "The Constitution of the United States is a marvelous document for self-government by Christian people. But the minute you turn the document into the hands of non-Christian people and atheist people, they can use it to destroy the very foundations of our society. And that's what's happening." ("700 Club," Dec. 30, 1981)....

Robertson startled those not already familiar with his view of the law in an interview with the editorial board of *The Washington Post* (June 27, 1986). Robertson argued that "A Supreme Court ruling is not the law of the United States. The law of the United States is the Constitution, treaties made in accordance with the Constitution and laws duly enacted by the Congress and signed by the president. And any of those things I would uphold totally with all my strength, whether I agreed with them or not."

Robertson claimed that the court's decision in *Roe v. Wade,* which legalized most abortions, was not the law of the land because it was based on "very faulty law." He added that as a private citizen, "I am bound by the laws of the United States and all 50 states...(but) I am not bound by any case or any court to which I myself am not a party....I don't think the Congress of the United States is subservient to the courts....They can ignore a Supreme Court ruling if they so choose."...

Robertson's views amount to nothing less than an endorsement of anarchy. What Robertson says, in effect, is that neither private individuals, presidents, nor members of Congress are bound to obey or enforce laws with which they disagree. If that is the case, the rule of law disappears. As president, Robertson would be free, for example, to work to reverse *Roe v. Wade,* but he would not have the option of not enforcing it....

Robertson has added one final twist to his constitutional theory: if all else fails, let God do it. In a speech to the National Right to Life Committee in Denver, he said abortion opponents could look to "the wonderful process of the mortality tables" to change the make-up of the court and bring about a new decision on abortion. Robertson stopped just short of praying for the death of Supreme Court justices with whom he disagrees, as other fundamentalists have done; but he is only a small step away....

Pat Robertson's views on the American legal system are not the views of a conservative who merely differs on key matters of judicial interpretation; they are the views of a radical who wants to emasculate the courts as a barrier to the exercise of the brute force of a majority scornful about the rights of the minority.

Education

Pat Robertson is not satisfied with attempting to remake the American judicial system; he is also taking aim at the public school system. He says "There are two major elites who are working in conjunction to take away the religious heritage from our nation. . . .The first is the educational elite. . . . In league with them are many people in the judicial system, the legal system." ("700 Club," Oct. 5, 1981).

America's public schools are more dangerous than "any place else," Robertson says ("700 Club," Nov. 29, 1982), because "the public schools are actually agencies for the promotion of another religion, which is the humanist religion." ("700 Club," Oct. 2, 1981). . . .

"The ultimate solution," Robertson says, "is that we have to work to get the state out of the business of educating kids at the primary and secondary levels, and get that education back in the hands of the parents where it belongs." ("700 Club," Oct. 2, 1981).

One target of Robertson's attack on public education is the National Education Association (NEA). In an attack on the NEA, he said "The teachers who are teaching your children . . . are not necessarily nice, wonderful servants of the community. They are activists supporting one party and one set of values and a number of the values which they espouse are: affirmative action, ERA, gun control legislation, sex education, illegal teachers's strikes, nuclear freeze, federal funding for abortions, decriminalization of marijuana, etc." ("700 Club," November 20, 1984). . . .

As long as there are public schools, Robertson believes, they should teach Creationism, the fundamentalist alternative to evolution. Robertson also charges that American textbook publishers are part of a plot against religion. . . .

To Pat Robertson, the only education is indoctrination in fundamentalist tenets; anything else is the work of the devil.

Women's Rights and Family Life

Life would be the way it is supposed to be again, Pat Robertson believes, if only women would return to their proper place in society. He summarizes his beliefs about marriage and family life in *Answers:*

"The apostle Paul, writing to the church of Ephesus, laid down some very good guidelines for husbands and wives. To the men, he said 'Husbands, love your wives, just as Christ also loved the Church and gave himself for it.' To the women, he said 'Wives, submit to your own husbands, as to the Lord.' That kind of relationship brings about a lack of tension in marriage.''. . .

Robertson has frequently elaborated on this view on television. For example, he offers this advice to women trying to convert their husbands: ''But women, one little remark. Please don't make your husbands think that in order to accept Jesus Christ, they have to submit to you, because no macho man wants to do that. They'll submit to Jesus, but they kind of like to be the head of the household. And that's scriptural. And that's the way it should be.'' (''700 Club,'' Dec. 10, 1982). . . .

Conclusion

For those who take the time to examine Pat Robertson's worldview in his own words, it is clear that he is an extremist. He claims to work miracles and identifies himself with God and those who disagree with him with Satan—or with ideologies he says are Satanic, like atheism, communism, Nazism, or ''secular humanism.''

Robertson cites a divine mandate for specific political objectives from his reading of the Bible and from his personal conversations with God. He would obliterate the separation of church and state and the separation of powers; he would dismantle the federal courts, the public schools, the Social Security system, the Federal Reserve Board, and government social programs, leaving the federal government with nothing to do except advocate sectarian beliefs, fight communists, and guarantee the government securities that God told him to buy.

WHAT IS RELIGIOUS BIAS?

This activity may be used as an individualized study guide for students in libraries and resource centers or as a discussion catalyst in small group and classroom discussions.

Many readers are unaware that written material usually expresses an opinion or bias. The skill to read with insight and understanding requires the ability to detect different kinds of bias. Political bias, race bias, sex bias, ethnocentric bias, and religious bias are five basic kinds of opinions expressed in editorials and literature that attempt to persuade. They are briefly defined below.

5 Kinds of Editorial Opinion or Bias

SEX BIAS—The expression of dislike for and/or feeling of superiority over a person because of gender or sexual preference

RACE BIAS—The expression of dislike for and/or feeling of superiority over a racial group

ETHNOCENTRIC BIAS—The expression of a belief that one's own group, race, religion, culture, or nation is superior. Ethnocentric persons judge others by their own standards and values.

POLITICAL BIAS—The expression of opinions and attitudes about government-related issues on the local, state, national, or international level

RELIGIOUS BIAS—The expression of a religious belief or attitude

Guidelines (Part A)

Evaluate the statements below by using the method indicated.

Check ✔ the letter [R] in front of any sentence that is an example of religious opinion or bias. Check ✔ the letter [N] in front of any sentence that is not an example of religious opinion or bias.

☐ R   ☐ N   1. The government should regulate television ministries.

☐ R   ☐ N   2. People who contribute to television ministries deserve full disclosure as to how their money was spent.

☐ R   ☐ N   3. Televangelists should not become involved in politics.

☐ R   ☐ N   4. Televangelists are unable to exercise the restraint and responsibility required to avoid federal regulation.

☐ R   ☐ N   5. People should ignore televangelists and give instead to churches and charitable institutions at home.

☐ R   ☐ N   6. Our Constitution prevents the government from regulating television ministries.

☐ R   ☐ N   7. If God came down to earth, he would not be on television asking for money.

☐ R   ☐ N   8. Televangelists have forgotten the poor and have spent their millions on cathedrals.

☐ R   ☐ N   9. Christian television is a powerful and positive force for millions of people.

☐ R   ☐ N   10. If televangelists had a personal relationship with God, they would ask for peace in the world and not for money.

☐ R   ☐ N   11. Religious broadcasters should be serving God, not glorifying themselves.

☐ R   ☐ N   12. Televangelists are honest servants of God and are able to regulate their ministries by themselves.

☐ R   ☐ N   13. We should not play God and judge the televangelists. We should trust them and send them our money.

☐ R   ☐ N   14. The Bible says that televangelists should be above reproach.

☐ R ☐ N 15. The Scriptures demand that television ministries be open and accountable.

☐ R ☐ N 16. God must purge His church of all wrong-doing ministers.

☐ R ☐ N 17. Christian faith has political implications, and televangelists have a right, even a responsibility, to help shape the direction of their nation.

☐ R ☐ N 18. Jesus had no place to lay his head, but televangelists sleep in mansions.

☐ R ☐ N 19. Jesus gave all he had to the poor; today's televangelists use money to build their empires.

☐ R ☐ N 20. Partisan political power is no fit replacement for the power of God upon which gospel preachers must finally rely.

☐ R ☐ N 21. One cannot be a humble servant of God, yet live in an ostentatious way.

Guidelines (Part B)

1. See how many factual statements you can locate in the 21 items listed above.

2. Make up one-sentence statements that would be an example of each of the following: *sex bias, race bias, ethnocentric bias, political bias, and religious bias.*

3. From any of the readings in this publication, locate at least three statements that reflect religious opinion or bias.

CHAPTER 4

ECONOMIC AND SOCIAL JUSTICE

145

19

ECONOMIC AND SOCIAL JUSTICE

CHURCHES AND THE SOCIAL ORDER: THE POINT

Edmund A. Opitz

The Reverend Edmund A. Opitz is a member of the staff of The Foundation for Economic Education, a seminar lecturer, and author of the book, Religion and Capitalism: Allies, Not Enemies. *Opitz's article appeared in* The Freeman, *the monthly publication of The Foundation for Economic Education (FEE). FEE is a nonpolitical educational champion of private property, the free market, and limited government.*

Points to Consider:

1. Why does the author describe the proclamations of various churchmen "the Socialist Party platform in ecclesiastical drag"?
2. Define environmentalism. Define materialism.
3. Compare and contrast capitalism, socialism, and communism.
4. Explain why capitalism creates large disparities in income.

Edmund A. Opitz, "Churches and the Social Order," *The Freeman*, August 1986, pp. 286-293.

It is a sad paradox indeed that the secular program, promoted by church hierarchies to alleviate poverty, has caused poverty in every society which has tried it. The only way to alleviate poverty in a nation is to increase productivity; and increased productivity is generated only by an economy of free men and women. Freedom is an essential part of the church's business. Freedom is a blessing in itself, and it's a double blessing, for prosperity follows freedom.

The Church Plays an Important Role in Human Life

It was once the unwritten rule in polite society that two topics have no place in civilized conversation: religion and politics. It was ill-bred to discuss religion; it was gauche to talk politics. But times have changed. We live in a different and more open age. Now we discuss religion for political reasons, and we talk politics for religious reasons! The Bishops issue a Letter; the highest dignitaries of the various denominations pronounce on matters of government and business. The people behind these proclamations represent only a tiny minority of the total church membership, but they presume to speak for everyone. What they say is, in effect, the Socialist Party platform in ecclesiastical drag.

These ecclesiastical documents focus on an economic malaise: poverty—the poverty of the masses, especially the masses of the Third World. Churchmen profess to know the cause of this poverty. Third World poverty is caused by the wealth of the capitalistic nations; *they* are poor because *we*, in becoming wealthy, have pauperized them. Likewise, within our own nation the wealth of those who are better off is gained at the expense of those who are made worse off in the process. These are the typical allegations: the rich get richer by making the poor poorer.

Ecclesiastical myopia views the market economy—or capitalism—as an evil system which, by its very nature impoverishes the many as the means by which the few are enriched. The suggested cure for these differentials in wealth is to use government's power to tax to exact tribute from the rich, and then distribute the proceeds to the poor—minus the cost to the nation of these wealth transfers. Robin Hood robs the rich to pay the poor, but Robin takes his cut!

It is as if these churchmen had swallowed the current secular agenda to which they have merely added oil and unction; as if social reform were the end, religion the mere means; as if religion has little more to offer modern men and women beyond what they can get from contemporary liberalism or socialism. The church has a more important role to play in human life, as I shall suggest in the course of this article. . . .

147

The Pull of Public Opinion

Churchmen in every age are tempted to adopt the protective coloration of their time; like all intellectuals, churchmen are verbalists and wordsmiths; they are powerfully swayed by the printed page, by catch words, slick phrases, slogans, and bumper stickers. In consequence, they are pulled first this way then that by whatever currents of public opinion happen at the moment to exert the greatest power over their emotions and imagination. Today, it is the powerful gravitational pull of "environmentalism."

I'm using the word environmentalism as a label for the belief that the human species is nothing but what external conditions have made us, that we are the victims of circumstances, that our lives are determined by forces we can barely understand, let alone control. . . .

Environmentalism exerts a powerful attraction today over intellectuals of all creeds. It is the ideology of Marxists and non-Marxists alike that men and women are the mere end products of nature and society— responsible men and women no longer—and that social engineering can construct a perfect society out of defective human units. Environmentalism has the cart before the horse; it is dehumanizing.

If there is a disorder in our society it follows that there is disorder within our very selves, in our faulty thinking and erroneous beliefs, in our misplaced loyalties and misguided affections. Disharmony in our personal lives will result in conflict and frictions in society. This is why serious religion has traditionally focused on the inward and the spiritual, on the mind and conscience of individual persons, to make them responsible individuals. The premise is that only right beliefs rightly held can produce right action. The good society emerges only if there is a significant number of people of intellect and character; and the eleva-

148

tion of character is the perennial concern of genuine religion, in league with education and art.

But the modern world views the matter differently. The modern world assumes that the human species is the mere end product of external forces; a product, first of all, of physics and chemistry—our natural environment; and a product, secondly, of the particular society in which an individual happens to live. The basic assumption is that man's character is made *for* him, by others; no individual is really responsible for himself. It is only necessary, then, for "the others" to acquire political power and use it to create social structures designed to produce a new humanity. Transform external arrangements and—according to this ideology—it matters little if men and women remain unregenerate; they will behave correctly because their institutions have programmed them to act according to the blueprint. This is the modern heresy.

Christianity, rightly understood, stands for a society with such basic features as personal responsibility, equal justice under the law, and maximum freedom for every person—the kind of society envisioned by the 18th-century Whigs like Burke, Madison, and Jefferson. Such a social and political order as the Whigs had in mind lays down the conditions in a nation which permit the operation of one kind of an economic order only, the free market economy—later nicknamed capitalism. . . .

Millions of people during the 20th century have turned away from the traditional religious faiths of the West—Christianity and Judaism—

149

to embrace some form of secular religion, such as communism or socialism. The prevailing world view in our time is not Theism—the belief that mind and spirit are rock-bottom realities in the universe; it is Materialism—the belief that basic reality is composed of nothing else but particles of matter.

Materialism is explicit wherever Marxism is the official creed, but it is implicit almost everywhere else. Begin with the Marxist premise of Dialectical Materialism—or any other variety of Materialism—and some form of totalitarianism logically follows. Such a society reduces human persons to minions of the state, to be used and used up in the utopian endeavor to bring about the classless society of the communist pipe dream. Christian doctrine, by contrast, makes the individual person central. His role in life is to serve the highest value he can conceive—God; the modest role of the political order is to provide maximum freedom for all persons in order that we, as created beings, may achieve our proper destiny. . . .

A Spotty Record

The history of the church during the past 2,000 years is a spotty record, with many ups and some downs. There have been glorious epochs, and there have been periods which make for melancholy reading. Occasionally, the church has sanctioned tyrannous political rule; from time to time it has lent its support to persecutions, inquisitions, and crusades. As an arm of the state, or as a tool of the state, it has betrayed its sacred task while it pursued secular goals like wealth and power.

In the 20th century segments of ecclesiastical officialdom and councils of churches demand legislation to transfer wealth from one group of citizens to another. They work for a collectivist economic order planned, controlled, and regulated by government. The intended aim is to overcome poverty and feed the hungry; the means is the planned economy, otherwise labeled socialism, collectivism, the new deal, or whatever. Whatever the label, the planned economy puts the nation in a strait jacket; the planned economy, however noble the intentions of the planners, is the road of serfdom, as F. A. Hayek demonstrated in a landmark book written some 40 years ago.

A planned economy forcibly directs the lives of individual men and women, and to do so the state must deprive people of their earnings which they would otherwise use to direct their own lives. Nation after nation during the 20th century has gone in for political planning of the economy and the results have been disastrous; where the planning has been strictly enforced, as in communist nations, the result has been a nation ill housed, ill fed, and ill clothed. It is a sad paradox indeed that the secular program, promoted by church hierarchies to alleviate poverty, has caused poverty in every society which has tried it. The only way to alleviate poverty in a nation is to increase productivity; and increased productivity is generated only by an economy of free men and women. Freedom is an essential part of the church's business. Freedom is a blessing in itself, and it's a double blessing, for prosperity follows freedom.

The socialists, until recently, have claimed the high moral ground. Their boast is that only socialists—or liberals—really care about people. What nonsense! Every person of good will wants to see other people better off; better housed, better fed, better clothed, healthier, better educated, with finer medical care, and all the rest. The dispute between socialists and believers in the free economy is not so much over the goals as over the means by which these goals may be met. The socialist's means—his command economy—will not achieve the goals he says he wants to reach; socialism makes the nation worse off: poorer in material wealth, and poorer in every other respect as well.

There is another route for churchmen to take, a way that leads to more freedom for people in society, rather than less freedom. Freedom is at the heart of the gospel message, and the true genius of our religion was proudly proclaimed by our forebears. . .

Man's will is uniquely free; that's the way God made us. We are free beings precisely in order that each person shall be responsible for his own life and therefore accountable for his action. It is by acts of will, acts of choice, exercised daily over the course of a lifetime that each of us becomes the person we have the potential to be. Each person is by nature self-controlling; each person is in charge of his own life.

The free society, then, is our natural habitat; freedom in the relations of persons to each other accords with human nature. The tactic of freedom in the business and industrial sectors is the free market economy; the free choice economic system corresponds to the freely choosing creature that each of us is. . . .

Because we are flawed creatures as well as free, we occasionally break the law, and so we need an umpire to interpret and, if necessary, enforce the rules. We refer to this umpire function as the political order—government, the police power, the law. And we have the courts, where honest differences of opinion may be examined and resolved.

The Productivity of Capitalism

The free market economy, or private property order, or capitalism—if you like—is, by common agreement, the most productive economic order. In fact, it's the *only* productive economic order. Socialism in a given country lives by exploiting the previous productive economy of that country, and when that gives out, socialist nations live on largess from capitalist nations.

The incredible productivity of capitalism is generally admitted, even by its critics; it's the way the wealth gets distributed that they complain about. What's wrong about capitalism, the critics charge, is that some

151

people in our society have enormous income while other people have to get by on a mere pittance. . . .

Part of the answer is that in a free society—a social order characterized by equal freedom under the law—the market place becomes a showcase for popular folly, ignorance, superstition, bad taste, and stupidity. The market, in other words, is individual free choice in action, and no one is pleased with everyone else's choices. But our displeasure is a price we must learn to pay if we are to enjoy the blessings of liberty. We must stand firmly behind the processes of freedom, even though we can barely stand some of the products of freedom. So let's stop wringing our hands; let's try to be tolerant, and let's get on with our lifelong task of setting a better example of what freedom means.

Remember that no one is *forced* to pay over good money to watch a sporting event; no one *has* to listen to some hyperkinetic young man howl and gyrate in public places to the accompaniment of amplified sound. . . .

Setting a Good Example

Let me emphasize the fact that the free market economy rewards each participant according to the value willing consumers attach to his offering of goods and services. . . .

It is a solid truth, I believe, that you cannot build a free society out of just any old kind of people. A free society is built around a nucleus of people of superior intellect and integrity who are, at the same time, cognizant of economic and political reality. You need people who love God and their neighbor; people of understanding and compassion; people with enduring family ties. Our schools and our churches should be producing people of this caliber, for it is the function of education and religion—in the broad sense of both terms—to make us better and wiser men and women. When we have a significant number of wise and good people living lives of a quality high enough to deserve a free society we'll *have* a free society. All the rest of us, riding on their coattails, will reap the rich blessings of liberty.

20 ECONOMIC AND SOCIAL JUSTICE

CHURCHES AND THE SOCIAL ORDER: THE COUNTERPOINT

James D. Von Dreele

The following reading, by the Reverend James D. Von Dreele, appeared in engage/social action, *a monthly publication of the General Board of Church and Society of The United Methodist Church. Reverend Von Dreele wrote this article in his capacity as rector of St. Matthew's Episcopal Church in Homestead, Pennsylvania.*

Points to Consider:

1. What is the "Babylonian captivity" of today's American church?
2. Define the Denominational Ministry Strategy. What purpose does it serve?
3. Explain what happened prior to and after the mass withdrawal of money from the Mellon Bank.
4. Why does the author believe today's church is unable to act like the prophets?

James D. Von Dreele, "Wielding the Sharp Edge of the Gospel: Pittsburgh Prophetic Ministry," *engage/social action*, October 1987, pp. 12-17. Reprinted with permission.

The institutional church seems quite content to live in comfort without exercising any strong prophetic challenge against the destructive forces of this world and seriously challenging institutions that cause the oppression of millions of people.

A number of years ago William Stringfellow described the current crisis of American Christianity as a "Babylonian Captivity" in his book *An Ethic for Christians and Other Aliens in a Strange Land* (Word 1973). As the biblical record makes clear, many of the exiled Jews were quite happy in the decadence of Babylon and had no desire to return to Jerusalem and the faith of their forefathers, Abraham, Isaac, and Jacob. The enticements of that foreign land seduced most of the people.

The "Babylonian captivity" of the American church today is more subtle but no less real as we see the church operating with the secular values of image, success, money, and even unwittingly becoming apologists for the very forces destroying people and communities. The institutional church is quite content to live in comfort without exercising any strong prophetic challenge against the destructive forces of this world.

In fact, the church today congratulates itself on how well it gets along with politicians and corporations—the power structure—"to get things done." It congratulates itself on how well it performs the ministry of helping those in trouble while refusing to challenge seriously the institutions that cause the suffering and oppression of millions of people. It does not see the obvious forms of institutionalized evil in our society. The church always faces the danger of losing the sharp edge of the gospel (the prophetic) when it is captured by the "principalities and powers" of this world. That is what has happened in Pittsburgh.

A Case in Point: Pittsburgh

The corruption of the church's ministry, both priestly and prophetic, can be seen in the church's response to the unemployment crisis in Pittsburgh over the last six years. This is the story of how some clergy and laity decided to exercise prophetic ministry for the sake of the unemployed and how not only the power structure but also the institutional church and its leaders attempted to destroy this ministry.

In 1982 a network of pastors and congregations known as the Denominational Ministry Strategy (DMS) sought ways to minister to the unemployed. DMS worked as an ecumenical ministry of five denominations in the Pittsburgh area (Lutheran, Episcopal, United Methodist, United Church of Christ, and Presbyterian).

Our first response was to organize food, clothing and job banks, job placement services, on-site feeding programs, financial management planning, support groups, mothers' day out programs, and other tradi-

A HUGE SUM OF MONEY

The money required to provide adequate food, water, education, health, and housing for everyone in the world has been estimated at $17 billion a year. It is a huge sum of money...about as much as the world spends on arms every two weeks.

Cecilia McCall, WREE-VIEW of WOMEN, *Summer 1986*

tional caring programs. Relentlessly, unemployment continued to rise as thousands more were laid off from plants in the Monongahela and Ohio River valleys.

In Mon Valley, employment went from 26,000 in 1979 in six USX (formerly US Steel) mills to 2,000 or so before the strike last summer. The real permanent job loss in the steel industry in the Mon Valley now equals over 100,000! These figures do not include hundreds of businesses that went under because of the depressed economy.

In December 1982, DMS petitioned then Governor Thornburg to declare the Mon Valley a "disaster area." The day before Christmas he informed us that would be impossible, even though the state statutes did provide help for such "manmade" disasters.

Since the politicians would not help, we visited their corporate sponsors to ask them to convince the politicians to help the people. (Corporate PAC groups contribute about 80 percent of all campaign monies on the federal level.) They turned a deaf ear. Mellon Bank, with $23 billion in assets, told us that it had "very little influence over the politicians."

At that same time Mellon and other major banks were pushing advantageous legislation in Congress to open up interstate banking. In response to this roadblock, DMS began a pledge campaign to move money out of a Mellon Bank and into banks that would invest in jobs in the Mon Valley.

In the midst of this organizing campaign Mellon Bank made a fateful decision. With two other local banks, Mellon called in a $20 million dollar loan to Mesta Machine (the foremost manufacturer of steel mill rolling equipment in the world) and forced Mesta into bankruptcy.

This incident focused the fight over unemployment. While Mellon Bank was foreclosing on Mesta, the bank had been loaning millions overseas, including over $100 million to Mesta's competitor in Japan, Sumitomo Industries (1977,79). Adding insult to injury, Mesta never paid the last three weeks of wages to the men ($500,000) and had cut off their medical and life insurance secretly two months before.

155

Photograph by Mary Harrison, Harrison Photography, 824 Neville Ave., Green Bay, WI 54303. Reprinted with permission.

Withdrawal of Money from Mellon

DMS in combination with the Network to Save the Mon/Ohio Valley and other community groups organized a mass withdrawal of money from the Mellon Bank on June 6, 1983 (D Day-Disinvestment Day). This action was seen across the nation on the nightly network news and Mellon Bank was clearly embarrassed by this tactic.

Two days after the bank withdrawal, the Mesta workers got their back pay! The tactic worked. But within a week of this action, the Lutherans and Episcopalians disavowed any connection with DMS and withdrew all funding, at the behest of the corporate leaders in the denominations. The United Methodists, Presbyterians, and UCCs dropped out of sight as well.

The church leaders reacted with horror when we focused clearly upon the main cause of unemployment in Pittsburgh—Mellon Bank through its disinvestment from the manufacturing base in the river valleys. Obviously, we touched too close to the heart of our denominational leaders' base—the corporations.

Within several months major reaction hit. The organizational trainer and the Lutheran bishop's assistant for urban ministry were both fired, as well as another assistant a few months later. Six DMS pastors faced well-organized attacks against their ministries. Three pastors went through major parish splits but in the end preserved their ministries. However, three others were forced out.

Pastors Douglas Roth of Trinity Church (Clairton) and Daniel Solberg of Nativity Church (Allison Park) were arrested and removed from their churches when they defied the Lutheran Synod's order to vacate their pulpits because of their DMS activities for the sake of the unemployed. Each spent over four months in prison.

Pastor Roth's council members remained in the church in defiance of another court order, which gave the church to the Synod, and they were arrested by riot-clad police and sentenced to one to two months in prison. The attorneys for Bishop May and the Lutheran Synod in all the court proceedings were none other than Reed, Smith, Shaw, and McClay—Mellon Bank's law firm of record for well over 100 years!

Not once in all the church disciplinary hearings against these pastors did the Lutheran Synod ever refer to scripture or theology. When challenged by DMS, the Synod used only the constitutions, Roberts' Rules of Order, and court injunctions prepared by Mellon Bank's attorneys.

The scriptural/theological/confessional crisis of the local and national Lutheran Church centers on their total disregard of the Bible in response to DMS and the prophetic ministry of its pastors. To rely on injunctions of secular courts to settle deep theological issues is in itself heretical. By operating totally on secular values with courts and lawyers to settle a major theological challenge to its ministry, the Lutheran Church violated Scripture and its own Lutheran Confessions.

Much of the media coverage over the last three years has centered on the Lutherans, but the biblical crisis we see transcends the Lutherans. It is in all denominations. By and large the church does not and can not act like Christ and the prophets. Why?

(1) Prophets were hated in their own country. Church people today want to be liked and accepted, not hated.

(2) Prophetic acts are never acceptable or popular, especially to those in power. These acts will always cause reaction with those doing the worst evil.

(3) Prophetic acts are by nature shocking. The Bible is full of examples: Isaiah running naked, the plagues against Egypt, turning over the money changers' tables, sending 2,000 pigs over the cliff, disrupting the silver smith's trade, disrupting worship in the synagogues.

DMS's prophetic acts (tactics) pale before the power of the biblical experience. We have used pennies, fish, skunk oil, and lots of humor. Our critics' "Alice-in-Wonderland" logic claims that these are violent tactics, yet these acts have often prevented major violence by the unemployed to whom we minister.

Major Learnings

(1) Invariably, church groups dealing with major social problems get pulled into corporate/political alliances which neutralize the fight against the evil. The local and religious press then does feature stories on how well these groups have accomplished their goals and "worked within the system."

(2) Mass movements for social change do not happen in this country unless the top institutional leaders move with them. That does not seem likely right now. South Africa is a case in point. Church leaders decry *apartheid* while their church pension funds continue in South African investments because of "fiduciary responsibilities" to the pensioners. This double talk undermines the theological and moral legitimacy of the church's witness. It cannot act strongly.

(3) Within the church there are forces which will confuse people and neutralize any strong prophetic action. . . .

Prophetic ministry does not depend upon mass movements to accomplish its ministry. In DMS we give hope to small congregations throughout the country so that they can be faithful to the gospel and force major changes for the sake of the people to whom they minister.

ECONOMIC AND SOCIAL JUSTICE

POVERTY AND THE ROLE OF THE CHURCH

The Coalition on Revival

The Coalition on Revival (COR) is a network of evangelical leaders from every major denominational and theological perspective who share a vision for and a commitment to revival, renewal, and reformation in Church and society in America.

This reading is excerpted from one in a series of COR documents. COR believes these documents set forth fundamental, non-negotiable Biblical principles governing major areas of human life and activity.

Points to Consider:

1. According to the COR, why do people suffer?
2. Explain why the COR gives primary responsibility for helping the hurting to individuals and the church. Describe the civil government's role in helping the hurting.
3. How does the COR hope to break the cycle of poverty?
4. Describe the church's role in helping the poor and suffering.

This essay is excerpted from the preface to *The Christian World View of Helping the Hurting,* edited by Gladys Dickelman and Robert Martin, copyright 1986, The Coalition on Revival. Used by permission. The complete document is available from The Coalition on Revival, 89 Pioneer Way, Mountain View, California 94041.

***It is foolish to expect our government to lead the way
in providing creative, constructive, and nurturing social
services.***

Suffering came to this world through Adam's and Eve's disobedience
to God and the resulting Fall of man and nature from their original state
of perfection as created by God. As a consequence, man is out of har-
mony with his Creator, with himself, with other men, and with nature.
Since then the earth has been plagued with violence, sickness,
disasters, death, and the suffering they bring.

Why do People Suffer?

Many suffer as a result of their own sinful choices in disobedience
to and rejection of God and His commands. Their sinful choices have
far-reaching, hurtful effects on the whole of their lives. They abuse their
bodies and minds with drugs, alcohol, sexual immorality, or neglect
of good health practices, and so suffer both physically and emotional-
ly. Likewise, suffering can come from broken relationships, stressful en-
vironments, internal strife not dealt with properly, or even demonic
attacks. Many in prison reap the consequences of their criminal
behavior, while others are captives of destructive additions springing
from their choices. Poverty can even result from rebellion against authority, sloth, lack of discipline and self control, or ignorance.

But others suffer without contributing directly to the causes of their
suffering. They are victims of outside forces like birth defects, accidents,
diseases, or sudden catastrophies (flood, earthquake, fire, drought, etc.).
Some suffer with the death of a family member or loved one. Others
are victims of human violence either in its institutional forms of governmental tyranny, war, and cultural prejudice, or in its individual forms of
crime, domestic and personal violence, or the "sins of the fathers."

Helping the Hurting is Not Civil Government's Responsibility

Governmental agencies have come to assume more and more of
the responsibility that once was in the hands of individuals, private
organizations, and churches for dealing with the hurting. The prevailing political philosophy leads us to believe that the hurting are the
government's responsibility.

The civil government does have some judicial, legal responsibility,
but as Dr. John Perkins* says, "It is foolish to expect our government
to lead the way in providing creative, constructive, and nurturing social

---

*Editor's note: Dr. John Perkins is the president and founder of Voice
of Calvary Ministries.

services." The government's poor track record shows it to be ineffective, often perpetuating the evils it seeks to resolve.

In contrast, the Bible gives primary responsibility for helping the hurting to individual Christians and the Church. We have a mandate from our Lord, and His promise to channel His great resources of love, wisdom, and energy through is to carry out our task. This is not an option, but a duty. We cannot abdicate our role as Jesus' hands, heart, and feet to our government or anyone else. "If a brother or sister is without clothing and in need of daily food, and one of you says to them, 'Go in peace, be warmed and be filled,' and yet you do not give them what is necessary for their body, what use is that"? (James 2:15, 16).

The driving motives and primary goals behind every helping act must be to obey and glorify God, to bring sinners to a saving knowledge of Christ, and to present every believer a mature person in Christ. The Body of Christ should be recognized as people who hear the cries of those in need and come to their aid. There should therefore be no division between evangelism and ministry to hurting people. There must be a witness of works of compassion if there is to be a true witness of the message of Jesus Christ. For Jesus said He came "to preach the gospel to the poor. . .to proclaim release to the captives, and recovery of sight to the blind, to set free those who are downtrodden, to proclaim the favorable year of the Lord" (Luke 4:18, 19). We must do likewise as His people, drawing on His power and His Word.

Help the Poor Become Self-sufficient

Our goal is to help the hurting to become able to help others, not to build our own egos by making ourselves indispensable. Our task is humbly and obediently to help others reach their potential of helping the hurting. We must not seek short-term solutions that perpetuate dependence and damage the dignity of those we "help." According to Perkins, to correct economic injustice, we must pursue development, empowering people to become self-sufficient through the power of the gospel. Victims of famine and war depend on our relief efforts, and we dare not neglect their needs. But the greater need is for development to break the cycle of poverty, so that today's receivers become tomorrow's givers.

This strategy should extend to many areas of hurt. The Bible teaches that it is more blessed to give than to receive; therefore we need to motivate and equip others to give so that they too may reap God's blessing.

Church Must be Haven for Justice

Although each Christian has personal responsibility for those who are suffering, individual action is not enough. The Church must be a haven, a minister of compassion, and a voice for justice. In addition to organizing united efforts to help the hurting, the Church must conform social, economic, legal, educational, medical, and governmental structures to Biblical order. Doing this would not only eliminate much suffering, but also enhance justice, righteousness, and compassion, increasing the effectiveness of the message of salvation. This requires that Christians in all walks of life cooperate in and through their local churches, and that local churches also work together.

Jesus said that the Law could be summed up in the commandments to love God and to love one's neighbor. We must not close our hearts to someone in need when we have the means to help. We cannot hope to eliminate all suffering in the world, even in one person's life; attempting it will engender only frustration and despair. The world is still fallen and the choice to sin is ever present. But we are called to significant, sacrificial acts of love, compassion, and obedience to God. "We know love by this, that He laid down His life for us; and we ought to lay down our lives for the brethren. But whoever has the world's goods, and beholds his brother in need and closes his heart against him, now does the love of God abide in him? Little children, let us not love with word or with tongue, but in deed and truth" (1 John 3:16-18).

22 ECONOMIC AND SOCIAL JUSTICE

POVERTY AND THE ROLE OF GOVERNMENT

The Lutheran Church of America and Others

This reading is an excerpt from a statement on the budget deficit and federal responsibility for the poor signed by 56 bishops of the Lutheran Church in America, the American Lutheran Church, and the Association of Evangelical Lutheran Churches.

Points to Consider:

1. Describe the particular government actions that have done little to help the poor.
2. Summarize the budgetary priorities for securing adequate funding for the poor.
3. Should people with earnings at or below the poverty line be required to pay federal income taxes? Why or why not?
4. Define the bishops' stance on federal funding for the poor.

The Lutheran Church of America, "A Message in Defense of the Poor," *Star Tribune,* 21 April 1985. Reprinted with permission.

The federal government has an appropriate role in meeting immediate needs, as well as in addressing the cause of poverty.

The nation's priorities are reflected in the budget choices it makes. This year, the soaring federal deficit makes particularly difficult the decision on how much revenue our nation must raise and how that revenue is to be spent. The church must speak for those whose pressing needs require not only private charity but also government action.

Government Must Help the Poor

Programs for the poor, which account for one-tenth of the federal budget, have been cut proportionately deeper than other programs. In addition, while the 1981 tax cut decreased the tax burden of many affluent Americans, persons at or below the poverty line have found themselves paying a greater percentage of their income in taxes. Due to these changes and to the effects of the recent recession, the standard of living of many poor Americans has deteriorated and their numbers have grown. Voluntary organizations have not been able to ensure that the needs of the poor are met.

Given the high rates of unemployment and poverty, a top budgetary priority should be securing adequate funding for human needs and income-maintenance programs, with standards ensuring that funds are targeted to those in greatest need.

Need Stronger Government Commitment

- No one in this prosperous country should be forced by economic conditions to go hungry, homeless, or without medical care. Even at current funding levels, federal benefits to poor families are often insufficient to provide adequately for their basic needs. We oppose any further reductions in the social safety net such as food stamps, Aid to Families with Dependent Children, Medicaid, Supplemental Security Income for the elderly poor, and low-income housing and energy-assistance programs. Eliminating cost-of-living adjustments or freezing funding for these programs will depress the standard of living of low-income families.

- Targeting special assistance to persons with special needs is good public policy. A dollar saved in program cuts today may result tomorrow in extended health-care costs, disruptions in earnings, unemployment, and other drains on our economy. Social services to keep families intact, child nutrition efforts, and health programs addressing the specific needs of low-income children are a crucial investment in our nation's welfare.

■ Persons with earnings at or below the poverty line should not pay federal income taxes. The 1981 cut in tax rates did little to address the special needs of the working poor. Failure to adjust for inflation the earned-income tax credit and other tax provisions means that the government is taxing away a greater and greater percentage of the dollars the poor desperately need to provide a minimal living standard.

■ Programs that address some of the root causes of poverty should be strengthened. These programs include education assistance for disadvantaged students and communities, job training, and legal services. Efforts to reduce the unacceptably high level of unemployment must be a major commitment of government.

■ The needs of the poor abroad cannot be ignored. The African tragedy highlights the need for both direct food aid and development assistance. The outpouring of donations to deal with famine indicates deep concern over the plight of the hungry abroad. However, the work of voluntary agencies complements but cannot replace government action in aid, trade, and development.

The Poor: Beyond Charities

The responsibility for addressing the needs of the poor is shared among individuals and institutions at every level of society. Private charity plays an important role and we encourage our own members to continue responding generously to the growing problems of poverty at home and abroad. But in our complex, highly mobile society, meeting the needs of the poor is beyond the capacity of charitable institutions. The federal government has an appropriate role in meeting immediate needs, as well as in addressing the causes of poverty. We value partnership between the voluntary and the government sectors in attempting to assist the poor to participate more fully in our economic life, but we strongly resist cuts in funding which undermine that partnership and seriously reduce the government's role in meeting pressing human needs.

Cartoon by Christian. Reprinted with permission of *The Internationalist*.

EXAMINING COUNTERPOINTS

This activity may be used as an individualized study guide for students in libraries and resource centers or as a discussion catalyst in small group and classroom discussions.

The Point

Handouts are not Biblical. Work is. That's why the government's current welfare system is a failure: it keeps people dependent and unproductive. We should cut the welfare rolls and help the disadvantaged develop skills that will enable them to work.

The Counterpoint

The Bible says 'Help Thy Neighbor.' Many of our "neighbors" in this country are denied the opportunity to work. It is our obligation, and our government's, to provide these people with money, food, clothing, and medical care until they are able to find work.

Guidelines

1. Examine the counterpoints.
2. Which argument do you agree with more and why?
3. Social issues are usually complex, but often problems become oversimplified in political debates and discussion. Usually a polarized version of social conflict does not adequately represent the diversity of views that surround social conflicts. Do the counterpoints oversimplify the issue of the government's role in helping the poor?

CHAPTER 5

RELIGION, AIDS, AND HOMOSEXUALITY

23

RELIGION, AIDS, AND HOMOSEXUALITY

HEALTH, PRIVACY, AND AIDS: THE POINT

Mark Smith

Mark Smith is the managing editor for the Liberty Report, *a monthly publication of the Liberty Federation. The Reverend Jerry Falwell is the founder of the Liberty Federation, an organization that focuses on broader issues than the Moral Majority—issues such as support for the "Star Wars" program, aid to the Nicaraguan contras and support for the governments of South Africa and South Korea.*

Points to Consider:

1. Why are health care workers having difficulty finding a strategy to contain the AIDS virus?
2. Summarize Congressman Dannemeyer's recommendations to control the spread of AIDS.
3. Explain why civil liberties organizations and homosexual groups oppose mandatory AIDS testing.
4. Why were Washington, D.C. police criticized for wearing rubber gloves while arresting AIDS demonstrators?

Mark Smith, "25,000 Dead and Still No Strategy for Containing the AIDS Epidemic," *Liberty Report,* October 1987, pp. 4, 12.

It is a civil right of the healthy to be protected from the grim and deadly disease.

Aids and Civil Rights

Health care workers nationwide are desperately trying to develop a strategy for containing the killer AIDS virus. That strategy is remaining as elusive as a cure for the disease.

The problem facing them is that they must balance the civil rights of the ill and the civil rights of the healthy.

For example, frustrated health care workers in Albany, New York had to determine whether they could order a woman infected with AIDS to discontinue engaging in sexual relations. Because she has not broken any state public health laws, they could not force her to accept their medical advice even though one of her sexual contacts had tested positive for the AIDS antibody.

And in Atlanta, Georgia, a woman with AIDS continued to breast feed her child despite pleas from health care workers to stop.

In California, Congressman William Dannemeyer has evoked cheers and jeers for his ambitious recommendations to control the spread of the disease.

"For public health purposes," Mr. Dannemeyer says, "anyone who is infected—a confirmed antibody positive—is considered contagious and should be handled accordingly.

"In order to stop the spread of this disease, it is essential that all forms of HIV infection be reportable to public health officials with confidentiality, but not anonymity."

Rep. Dannemeyer is also urging that routine testing "should be implemented under special situations." He wants to test couples applying for marriage licenses, pregnant women, immigrants, health care workers, prisoners, and those in drug treatment programs.

These recommendations are being made to counter staggering statistics: As many as 200 women per year in Baltimore, Maryland, alone give birth to AIDS infected children; more than 3,000 military persons carry the AIDS virus; hundreds of immigrants would test positive each year should a required test be mandated.

Time to Take Action

Rep. Dannemeyer and several other lawmakers have decided that it is time to act.

They propose that 1) physicians should be required to inform the sexual partners of someone who is infected, 2) existing laws that make this illegal or criminal should be eliminated, and 3) contact tracing of sexual partners should be practiced to the fullest extent that manpower allows.

These recommendations, however, are where the civil rights issues come into play.

"A Very Democratic Death"

Homosexual groups and civil liberties organizations, such as the American Civil Liberties Union (ACLU), have cried foul at suggestions that there be required testing in the gay community.

They fear that testing would result in public knowledge of a victim's condition, possible harassment, and discrimination.

And they are extremely skeptical of promises that confidentiality will be guaranteed in AIDS testing.

Rep. Dannemeyer responds: "In our major cities, the majority of homosexuals are infected with the AIDS virus. Many are still living like lemmings, more concerned about their sexual freedoms than their health.

"It is critical that we get the civil rights issue into perspective or we will all die a very democratic death. Protecting the civil rights of some while infringing on the civil rights of others is resulting in greater numbers of infected people."

None will deny that these are strong propositions, but Mr. Dannemeyer demands that "one must alarm and concern people enough to motivate change, then calm them down with an action plan to demonstrate how they can stay healthy. We must promote the concept of quality monogamy."

Widespread AIDS Testing

Mr. Dannemeyer, however, has certainly not made the strongest statements concerning AIDS on Capitol Hill.

"I may be the most radical person you'll talk to on this (AIDS). But somewhere along the line we're going to have to quarantine people with AIDS. We might as well face facts," said Sen. Jesse Helms (R-NC) on CBS television's "Face the Nation."

"I'm not all that concerned about confidentiality," he continued. "My aim is to protect people who are innocent."

Mr. Helms has introduced a bill in the Senate encouraging widespread testing for the AIDS virus—testing that will help identify hazardous activities of AIDS carriers, such as the following:

A Los Angeles man in June was charged with attempted murder after he sold his AIDS-contaminated blood.

"I know that AIDS can kill," the man was reported to have said to *USA Today.* "But I was so hard up for money I didn't give a damn."

Joseph Edward Markowski, 29, sold his blood up to 23 times in a six-month period.

And the list goes on.

"Homophobic" Actions

Small towns, large cities, and entire states have issued plans for blood testing for laws preventing AIDS carriers like Markowski from infecting unsuspecting victims. . . .

However, these actions are considered "homophobic" by homosexual groups who have begun a criticism campaign against persons attempting to preserve their own safety.

Washington, DC police were denounced in June after they wore rubber gloves while arresting demonstrators at an AIDS rally.

Police officials were convinced by local homosexual groups that the gloves were inappropriate during the arrests.

Such actions reinforce "misconceptions about how the AIDS virus is transmitted and could be harmful to efforts to educate the public about the deadly disease," a release from DC Mayor Marion Barry's office said.

That response to the donning of the protective gear, however, angered Officer Gary Hankins, chairman of the labor committee for the Fraternal Order of Police.

He told the *Washington Times*, "Frankly, I'm getting damned tired of the gay community's political arm-twisting to conform policy for their own interests instead of the safety of the community. . .and my police officers."

In Illinois, the bill requiring the state Department of Public Health to trace the sex partners of persons infected with AIDS, were called "some of the most coercive and counter-productive legislation in the United States" by a group of 60 state physicians.

We Need to Protect the Healthy

Beyond voluntary testing, civil liberty organizations and homosexual groups complain vigorously.

The voluntary test and continued education in safe sex practices is good, they say, but required tests and informing intimate contacts of a victim's infection or tracing those contacts is bad.

Nat Hentoff, writing in *The Village Voice* (New York's homosexual mouthpiece), probably shocked a few readers when he commented, "(If) identities (of AIDS victims) are known, the stigma can be crushing. It sure can. So can the death of someone who didn't know his or her lover had the virus. That is the very crux of the debate about testing: Is protecting privacy invariably worth the cost of another's life?

"Voluntary testing and education are essential but they are not always enough."

But only eight states now require victims of AIDS to be reported to state agencies.

"If a physician encounters a person with the virus for AIDS" in the other 42 states, says Rep. Dannemeyer, "he is not required to report that to public health authorities. And bear in mind, that is a noncommunicable venereal disease. But on the other hand, if a physician encounters a person with a curable venereal disease, such as syphilis or gonorrhea, the physician is required to report that to public health authorities."

The bathhouse culture of sexual promiscuity must stop and laws to ensure they stop—to ensure public health safety—must begin soon, says Mr. Dannemeyer.

It is a civil right of the healthy to be protected from the grim and deadly disease.

24 RELIGION, AIDS, AND HOMOSEXUALITY

HEALTH, PRIVACY, AND AIDS: THE COUNTERPOINT

Ira Glasser

Ira Glasser is the executive director of the American Civil Liberties Union (ACLU). The ACLU is a nonpartisan organization devoted to the defense of civil liberties in the United States. It supplies counsel and files legal briefs in important cases involving violations of civil liberties. In addition, its officials discuss problems of civil liberties with officials of the U.S. government and testify before legislative committees.

Points to Consider:

1. Explain why the ACLU has been criticized for its opposition to mandatory AIDS testing.
2. Why do public health officials (and the ACLU) favor voluntary AIDS testing?
3. Describe the ACLU's ideas for containing AIDS.
4. How many people would be falsely identified in widespread mandatory AIDS testing?

Unfounded fear often leads us to abandon our concern for individual rights and to embrace policies that falsely promise deliverance.

ACLU Not Opposed to Good Public Health Measures

The American Civil Liberties Union (ACLU) has been severely criticized for its opposition to compulsory testing for AIDS and to government efforts to identify and trace all sexual contacts of those suspected of harboring the AIDS virus.

It has been wrongly asserted that this organization has opposed "obviously good" public health measures in order reflexively to protect the right of privacy.

Actually, the ACLU sees no conflict between civil liberties and sound public health policies. Nor is it alone. Public health officials overwhelmingly oppose mandatory testing and contact-tracing. They believe that such programs would make it harder, not easier, to limit the spread of AIDS.

Scapegoats and Clear-cut Answers

People understandably panic when they first confront the policy issues related to AIDS. The disease is fatal, it has no cure or even a successful treatment, and it is communicable. Worse, it is heavily stigmatized by prejudice toward homosexuality.

In a situation of panic, and with an easily identified scapegoat group available, people often grasp at what seem to be simple and clear-cut answers—even if those answers are wrong.

So the assumption is intuitively made that forced testing will be effective in preventing the spread of the AIDS virus. In fact, this is a field in which coercion would almost certainly backfire.

Mandatory Testing Will Not Work

Our only protection against AIDS now is preventing the spread of the virus. Successful prevention efforts depend on reaching as many people as possible with accurate information about the disease and on persuading them to make appropriate changes in their behavior.

Mandatory testing would not achieve that end. It would only drive people away from health authorities, which is why most public health officials oppose it.

What public health officials want is more voluntary testing. And they want to be able to assure people who do come in that they will not face punitive sanctions like quarantine, or have their names entered into a government computer, or suffer the loss of jobs or housing or health insurance. Such consequences subvert the very efforts we need most strongly to promote.

175

Civil Liberties and Public Health

One of the greatest tragedies of AIDS is that so many have died because this disease and basic information about it have been forced into a medical underground. We desperately need to bring people forward, not drive them away.

It is for these reasons that the conflict between civil liberties and public health is often more perceived than real. The Centers for Disease Control, part of the U.S. Public Health Service, has just drafted a major set of recommendations for AIDS-related testing programs. Its major finding is that all such testing should remain voluntary. The surgeon general of the United States has taken the same position, as has the American Public Health Association and virtually every public health official in the country.

The ACLU's policy on AIDS is consistent with public health interests.

We favor broad access to testing on a voluntary basis, anonymously if possible but with confidentiality assured. We have filed lawsuits both to protect individual rights and to force the government to do more to educate the public about the risks of AIDS. We have also called for strong anti-discrimination laws to help counter the stigma and prejudice that has crippled much of the prevention work.

Don't Ignore Privacy

We do not apologize for our concern for traditional rights. Privacy is not something to be easily set aside during moments of hysteria. Nor is it merely an abstract legal principle to be debated and dissected by lawyers. Widespread mandatory testing of the general population, where the incidence of AIDS is still very small would inevitably result in a large number of false positives, perhaps as much as 28 percent, according to a forthcoming study from the Harvard School of Public Health. The consequences to those people falsely identified are not trivial and should concern us all.

Unfounded fear often leads us to abandon our concern for individual rights and to embrace policies that falsely promise deliverance. Mandatory testing and contact-tracing will not deliver us from the threat of

176

AIDS. To argue otherwise is counter-productive to both public health and civil liberties.

RELIGION, AIDS,
AND HOMOSEXUALITY

AIDS:
THE HOMOSEXUAL PLAGUE

David A. Noebel, Wayne C. Lutton,
and Paul Cameron

David A. Noebel is the president of Summit Ministries, a religious, educational Christian Leadership Training Center located in Manitou Springs, Colorado. He has also written The Homosexual Revolution.

Wayne C. Lutton is the director of Summit Research Institute. The Institute engages in research, writing, and lecturing on Biblical and moral issues affecting the Christian faith.

Paul Cameron is the chairman of the Family Research Institute in Lincoln, Nebraska.

All three authors have given official testimony and appeared on radio and television programs to discuss the AIDS issue.

Points to Consider:

1. Why do the authors disapprove of homosexual representation on various AIDS task forces?
2. Explain how the majority of people have contracted AIDS.
3. Define ethical humanism.
4. Describe the authors' position with regard to homosexuality.

David A. Noebel, Wayne C. Lutton, and Paul Cameron, *AIDS: Acquired Immune Deficiency Syndrome* (Manitou Springs, Co.: Summit Ministries, 1986), pp. 3-6.

How can there be a positive view of homosexuality? Its very practice is proving to be lethal.

Introduction

The United States faces a health crisis that has the potential of destroying our society.

It is called AIDS, Acquired Immune Deficiency Syndrome. The condition was initially known as GRID—Gay Related Immunodeficiency Disease—and was only rechristened AIDS after lobbying by homosexual medical activists (MS magazine, May 1983, p. 103).

Dr. William A. Haseltine, Harvard Medical School, says it is a problem that will not go away. "Every time we look at it," he says, "it looms larger so that now the shadow of this disease has begun to darken all our lives."

New York University's Dr. Alvin Friedman-Kine refers to the disease as the "plague of the millennium."

AIDS is the popular acronym for a disease caused by a retrovirus labeled HTLV-3, which stands for human T-lymphotropic virus type 3 (for a complete medical description see "The Immune System in AIDS" by Prof. Jeffrey Lawrence, Cornell University, *Scientific American,* December 1985, pp. 84-93; and JAMA's *Medical News* article "AIDS—associated Virus Yields data to Intensifying Scientific Study," November 22/29, 1985, pp. 2865ff.).

Unfortunately, retroviruses fasten mightily to the genetic material (DNA) of a person's immune cells. The virus also lodges in and infects the brain cells and central nervous system of its victims. It is a terrible, fatal, communicable disease. Its causes, course, and consequences must be faced squarely and honestly.

AIDS carries within itself the possibility of wreaking "a devastation such as has not been encountered on this planet in hundreds of years," warns Dr. Richard Restak, a Washington, D.C. neurologist. And Dr. Ward Cates of the U.S. Centers for Disease Control (CDC) categorically stated, "Anyone who has the least ability to look into the future can already see the potential for this disease being much worse than anything mankind has seen before.

The Gay Influence

The affected and infected already number in the millions and the Public Health Service has predicted that the fight against this disease could last 15 years or more. The December 1985 issue of *Scientific American* magazine places the number of people in this country alone who are now numbered among the AIDS risk group at "tens of millions." Dr. Malcolm Maclure, Harvard University, portrayed the future in this way: "Imagine full 747 jumbo jets crashing daily through 1990 and you grasp the possible scale of the AIDS epidemic to come."

179

The Public Health Service also admits that public information is "currently the only mechanism available to prevent infection."

Unfortunately, homosexuals sit on the very panels which are supposed to protect us from their most deadly disease. The American College Health Association, which plans to produce some recommendations and guidelines to combat AIDS on campus, has representatives of homosexual coalitions on its special 20-member AIDS task force. These coalitions and task forces have basically one object in mind: to preserve and protect homosexual behavior. Their influence can be seen in the newly developed AIDS guidelines drawn up by the National Education Association: "No student, school employee, or potential school employee shall be required to provide information as to his or her sexual orientation."

For anyone researching the subject of AIDS, however, one thing becomes immediately apparent—one's "sexual orientation" has a great bearing on the matter. "The mechanisms by which the disease is transmitted are very clear," says Dr. Anthony S. Fauci, director of the National Institute of Allergy and Infectious Diseases, "One is sexual predominantly homosexual contact in this country. This accounts for almost three quarters of the reported cases" (JAMA *Medical News,* November 22/29, 1985, p. 2867).

Homosexuality: A Lethal Practice

The truth is that homosexuality accounts for over 90 percent of the AIDS problem. Those afflicted with hemophilia have contracted AIDS from the infected blood donated by homosexuals. Contaminated blood donated by homosexuals has led to the spread of AIDS to innocent victims. And the vast majority of drug users who have AIDS were using needles contaminated by blood traced to homosexuals. Only about 6 percent of the adult cases of AIDS occur in persons who do not fall into any of the known high risk groups. And some of these could have been infected by insects, such as mosquitoes, that transferred blood from an AIDS carrier to a potential AIDS victim.

AIDS

Acquired Immune Deficiency Syndrome

SPECIAL REPORT

The nation's worst public health problem.
No one has ever recovered from the disease,
and the number of cases is doubling every year.
Fears are growing now since the AIDS plague is
spreading beyond homosexuals and other high-
risk groups to threaten the population at large.

Including an evaluation of the U.S. Surgeon General's
Report on AIDS

The authors of *AIDS: Acquired Immune Deficiency Syndrome* manage to sample and comment upon the best (and worst) that has been written about the progress of AIDS in the United States.

Since the homosexual revolution is part of the larger sexual revolution, those responsible for the revolution are determined to protect one of their most important allies. "The spirit of the age," says Jeffrey Hart, "regards disapproval of homosexuality as simple bigotry, and the liberal mentality is zealous in its efforts to protect homosexuals from any disagreeable consequences of their practices whether social, economic, or medical consequences.

In 1966 the National Organization of Women (NOW) was founded for the purpose of helping to bring about "a sex-role revolution for men and women which will restructure all our institutions: childbearing, education, marriage, the family, medicine, work, politics, the economy, religion, psychological theory, human sexuality, morality, and the very evolution of the race."

At its July 19-21, 1985 New Orleans National Convention NOW listed as one of its goals to "work for adequate and effective sex education programs that present a positive view of women's sexuality, and of lesbians and homosexuality." But how can there be a positive view of homosexuality? Its very practice is proving to be lethal.

The battle against AIDS, therefore, is not just a battle against the plague. It is battle against a philosophy—a philosophy that embraces homosexuality as an integral part of its ethic.

Ethical Humanism

Those combating the AIDS plague will soon discover that they are also fighting the National Education Association (NEA), the National Organization of Women (NOW), the American Civil Liberties Union (ACLU), and other groups involved in protecting homosexual conduct.

For example, those in Congress seeing ways to isolate and conquer AIDS are themselves being isolated by their fellow pro-homosexual Congressmen. The pro-homosexual constituency in Congress is primed to make sure that no anti-homosexual legislation surfaces no matter how fiercely the AIDS plague rages. This is not just a matter of stemming a plague, but a philosophy of life.

Ethical humanism has already determined that the Judeo-Christian ethic has been "too dour"—no longer providing sufficient pleasures for "the good life." Its laissez-faire ethical roots are based neither in God nor History, but simply in whatever makes men feel good. And the humanist bill of ethical rights very definitely includes homosexuality (as well as non-monogamous, heterosexual relationships).

Since ethical humanism has recently suffered a serious setback to its dogma from herpes, it wants to avoid another loss via AIDS. "For years," said Henry Fairlie, "liberals have been warned that they were trampling on the decent feelings of most ordinary people. But they casually have gone on with their effrontery, and now they have reaped their predictable regard. Will they learn even now?" (*New Republic,* January 31, 1981, p. 17.)

AIDS: A Homosexual Disease

There are essentially three major positions regarding the AIDS/homosexual plague: (1) Homosexuals must be allowed to carry on their sexual practices since it is their civil right to do so; (2) Homosexuals should voluntarily alter their sexual behavior by reducing their number of sexual partners or becoming monogamous, and by practicing various creative "safe sex" techniques; (3) Homosexuals should cease homosexual conduct, become celibate or change to heterosexuality; the homosexual subculture should be suppressed by being declared illegal under state sodomy laws.

Ethical humanism will opt for the first two alternatives. Unfortunately, the first alternative is the reality of our land today. Even states with sodomy laws can't legally curb homosexual behavior. Insightful men warned us about homosexual bathhouses and AIDS years ago, but even these dens of disease have yet to be closed.

The authors of this special report make no secret that they embrace the third position. It is because our society is divided over whether or not homosexual behavior is a civil right that AIDS has taken on such grave medical, religious, legal, and political overtones. It is our contention that homosexuality, like drug abuse, is not a civil right. It is not behavior meriting protection under the U.S. Constitution. In fact, it is conduct currently outlawed in 23 states, and which should be outlawed in all 50.

"In a healthy society," says Patrick J. Buchanan (White House Director of Communications), "homosexuality will be contained, segregated, controlled, and stigmatized."

Or as Daniel Bell put it, "When there is no restraint, when mere experience is the touchstone of what should be permitted, the impulse to explore everything, to seek all sensations. . . leads to debauchery, lust, degradation of others, and murder. The lesson they [the religions of the West] have all drawn is that a community has to have a sense of what is shameful, lest the community itself lose all sense of moral norms" (*The Cultural Contradictions of Capitalism,* 1976, p. 276-77).

Our society has gone in the opposite direction and now is suffering from an outbreak of homosexual veneral disease that already effects millions and could shake our nation to its very foundation. History contains examples of plagues having destroyed the greatness of previous civilizations (see William H. McNeill, *Plagues and People,* and Frederick F. Cartwright, *Disease and History*). Even Moses had to take extraordinary measures against a sexually transmitted disease that nearly destroyed early Israel (Numbers 25). . . .

As Dr. Jay A. Levy of the University of California, San Francisco, advises, "It is best to be prepared and expect the worst."

RELIGION, AIDS,
AND HOMOSEXUALITY

HOMOSEXUALITY
DOES NOT CAUSE AIDS

The American Lutheran Church

This reading is excerpted from an American Lutheran Church Mission Discovery Report. The American Lutheran Church is a member of the Lutheran World Federation, the World Council of Churches, and the Lutheran Council, U.S.A. The church conducts extension work (aid outside the church) in most parts of the continental United States and in 12 world mission areas.

Points to Consider:

1. What suggestion does the Vice President of Science and Technology of the American Medical Association offer for controlling the spread of AIDS?
2. How was AIDS initially portrayed in the United States? What problems has this created?
3. Why should the church confront issues of sexuality?
4. Define homophobia.

The American Lutheran Church, *AIDS: A Serious and Special Opportunity for Ministry* (Minneapolis, MN: Mission Discovery, July 1987), pp. 1-5.

Homosexuality does not cause AIDS. A virus causes AIDS.

Introduction

The eight-page Mission Discovery Report no. 9, AIDS: A Challenge to the Church . . . (March 1986) began with these words: **"Aids calls for an enormous amount of sanity, sensitivity, compassion, and level-headedness on behalf of the church and society at large."** This statement is as true today as it was then. The number of AIDS cases and deaths is living up to grave projections. From mid-January 1986 until mid-March 1987, the number of AIDS cases and deaths more than doubled. The AIDS pandemic is reaching into an increasing number of unsuspecting communities at an alarming rate.

A letter addressed to the General Secretary of the Lutheran Council in the U.S.A. from the Vice President of Science and Technology of the American Medical Association states the concern quite well:

> "The only way to control spread of the HIV virus is a massive educational effort to change sexual behavior in this country. In addition, education is needed in communities everywhere on how to care for AIDS patients, on the importance of screening tests for the virus, and on the absolute necessity that communities prepare for AIDS without stigmatizing it as a disease of homosexuals and drug abusers.

> "It is tempting to believe that AIDS will not reach most communities. This is wishful thinking. In many communities the HIV virus is already present, and it will reach others soon. Before this epidemic subsides, all of us will grieve in some personal way about AIDS— because of a loved one, a family member, a friend, or a business associate.

> "Preparing a community for problems like AIDS is not easy. It takes dedicated and enlightened guidance by community leaders."

The number of pastors reporting AIDS cases and deaths in their congregations and communities continues to increase. These reports come from communities both large and small. Pastoral concerns are wide and varied. Central to such reports and inquiries are concerns over ways and means to provide meaningful pastoral care to people with AIDS and their loved ones.

The challenge to the church continues the same as we suggested in Mission Discovery Report no. 9:

1. To get past the debate about how God views homosexuality.
2. To help the church and society understand that gay and lesbian people are worth caring for.

3. To demonstrate to gay and lesbian people that they are loved.
4. To get accurate and up-to-date information out to the public.
5. To make public discussion happen that faces up to the political, social, economic, health, religious, and ethical issues at every level of human interaction including the church, school, and government.
6. To carry out a compassionate and caring ministry to those whose lives have been, are, and will be affected by AIDS.
7. To grow in its understanding of who is included in the body of Christ.
8. To live out the resources of faith rather than to live fearfully. . . .

AIDS: A Serious and Special Opportunity for Ministry

Acquired Immune Deficiency Syndrome (AIDS) is **serious** and deadly. **It is serious** for those who contract it: at present there is no cure. **It is serious** for family members and friends of People With AIDS (PWA's) and People With Aids Related Complex (PWARC's), who struggle to care for their loved ones, and grieve at their loss. **It is serious** for our health care system, where increased demand for care strains existing resources. **It is serious** for our society as we sort out issues of individual rights and the need for public health protection. Finally **AIDS is a serious opportunity for the church** to understand what it means to minister in the name of Christ to those who have been, are, and will be affected by it.

Information about AIDS has become increasingly available. The bulk of material produced thus far has focused on medical facts about transmission and prevention. This is important and necessary informa-

tion. The medical implications are only one aspect of the effect of AIDS. There is also a growing need to consider the emotional, social, political, theological, and spiritual implications. . . .

Public Awareness of AIDS

AIDS was initially portrayed in this country as a disease limited almost exclusively to homosexual and bisexual males and intravenous drug abusers. This perception created a false sense of security for persons who did not regard themselves to be in such a so-called "high risk" group. It is now apparent that this initial perception was short-sighted. The virus that causes AIDS (called the Human Immunodeficiency Virus-HIV) does not distinguish between men and women, adults and children, rich and poor, gay and nongay, Christian and non-Christian. The reported and projected pattern of the spread of AIDS to groups other than the first two identified **does not mean** the virus has "spread to the general population." AIDS has **always been in** the "general population" where it is now manifesting itself more noticeably.

This means most people will find themselves involved in or touched by the AIDS epidemic in a variety of ways. Having personal friends or family with AIDS will become a more common experience. Friends, co-workers, or church members may have family members with AIDS. There are also people whose professional involvement includes caring for PWA's or PWARC's. News reports and social conversation are increasingly permeated with the subject. Encounters with people who are worried or frightened by the prospect of "catching AIDS" are on the increase. Requests for support or opposition of public policy proposals related to AIDS will be a common experience. The health care and insurance industries already are affected. All such realities will in turn affect everyone in ways we can't yet foretell. Such circumstances might make us angry, defensive, or afraid. It is important to recognize and deal with legitimate concerns without becoming paralyzed by irrational fear or bigotry. Two things should be remembered:

**There is no one to blame but the virus.
We are not powerless. . . .**

Confronting Issues of Sexuality

Ministry in the context of AIDS cannot avoid attitudes and feelings about sexuality. This subject has proven difficult enough under the best conditions.

If the people of a church are not accustomed to addressing issues of sexuality and relationships in the regular course of their life together, they are likely to have a difficult time doing so in this context.

Frank discussion of the facts involved is absolutely necessary, though many may feel it to be inappropriate in a church setting. In fact, there is no other agency or institution that should be as well-qualified. The church should have something to say regarding sex education in the home, churches, and schools, the destructive dynamics of homophobia, and intimacy and relationships. The discussion of sexuality and AIDS necessitates the use of the explicit language of sexuality. Responsible education for people about AIDS requires the use of words like "anal sex" and "condom" at some point. Many people may become disturbed or even angry if this is done. **Some people may die of AIDS if it is not.**

One major route of transmission for the AIDS virus is through sexual intercourse. Some people may be too embarrassed to discuss AIDS for this reason. A fearful response to the danger of AIDS has even created an atmosphere in which people have begun to equate sexual contact with death: "If you have sex, you will get AIDS and die, so don't have sex." To complicate the issue further, there is the multitude of fears and biases concerning homosexuality called **HOMOPHOBIA;** that is, fear, distress, and hostility toward gay and lesbian people. All together, this leaves a formidable tangle of emotions, fears, feelings, and facts for people to sort out. One doesn't have to approve of homosexuality to care for people who are ill. One doesn't have to be a homosexual to be concerned about the AIDS epidemic. One doesn't have to practice sexual abstinence in order to avoid AIDS.

Sexuality is a gift from God, meant to be enjoyed and used creatively. That will mean different things to different people. Like all gifts, it can be abused or damaged. When that happens, lives and relationships suffer. **God's response to our brokenness and suffering is healing and wellness, not punishment and disease.** Sexual intercourse does not cause AIDS. **Homosexuality does not cause AIDS. A virus causes AIDS.**

INTERPRETING
EDITORIAL CARTOONS

This activity may be used as an individualized study guide for students in libraries and resource centers or as a discussion catalyst in small group and classroom discussions.

Although cartoons are usually humorous, the main intent of most political cartoonists is not to entertain. Cartoons express serious social comment and important issues. Using graphics and visual arts, the cartoonist expresses opinions and attitudes. By employing an entertaining and often light-hearted visual format, cartoonists may have as much or more impact on national and world issues as editorial and syndicated columnists.

Points to Consider:

1. Examine the cartoon in this activity (see next page).

2. How would you describe the message of the cartoon? Try to describe the message in one to three sentences.

3. Do you agree with the message expressed in the cartoon? Why or why not?

4. Does the cartoon support the author's point of view in any of the readings in this publication? If the answer is yes, be specific about which reading or readings and why.

5. Are any of the readings in this publication in basic conflict with the cartoon?

PAT ROBERTSON

APPENDIX

This appendix presents the addresses and phone numbers of organizations that identify themselves as being both religious and conservative. The reader may find this information useful as a research tool for acquiring specific information about a particular group's religious philosophy and political agenda. This appendix was compiled from the data base of the People for the American Way.

American Bureau of Economic Research
P.O. Box 8204
Fort Worth, Texas 76124
(800) 527-8608, (817) 595-2691 in Texas

American Coalition for Traditional Values
122 C Street NW., Suite 850
Washington, D.C. 20002
(202) 628-2967
President: Dr. Tim LaHaye

American Family Association
(formerly National Federation for Decency)
P.O. Drawer 2440
Tupelo, Mississippi 38803
Executive Director: Don Wildmon

American Vision, Inc.
P.O. Box 720515
Atlanta, Georgia 30328
(404) 988-0555
Founder and President: Gary D. DeMar

Association of Christian Schools International
President: Dr. Paul A. Kienel

Bob Jones University
Greenville, South Carolina 29614
(803) 242-5100
Chancellor: Dr. Bob Jones, Jr. (BJU)

Calcedon
P.O. Box 158
Vallecito, California 95251
(209) 736-4365
Founder and President: Reverend R. J. Rushdoony

Campus Crusade for Christ (International & Inc.)
Arrowhead Springs
San Bernardino, California 92414
(714) 886-5224
President: Dr. William R. Bright

Christendom College
Front Royal, Virginia 22630
(703) 636-2908
President: Damion Fedoryka

Christian Action Council
422 C Street, NE
Washington, D.C. 20002

Christian Anti-Communism Crusade
P.O. Box 890: 227 E. Sixth Street
Long Beach, California 90801
(213) 437-0941
Founder and President: Fred C. Schwartz

Christian Broadcasting Network, Inc.
CBN Center
Virginia Beach, Virginia 23463
(804) 424-7777
President: Timothy Robertson

Christian Law Association
P.O. Box 3030
Conneaut, Ohio 44030
(216) 599-8900
President: Dr. Earl Little

Christian Voice, Inc.
P.O. Box 96541
Washington, D.C. 20077
Chairman: Robert Grant

Coalitions for America
721 Second Street
Washington, D.C. 20002
(202) 546-3003
National Chairman: Paul M. Weyrich
President: Curt Anderson

Concerned Women for America
122 C Street NW., Suite 800
Washington, D.C. 20001
(202) 628-3014
Chief Executive Officer: Beverly J. LaHaye

Coral Ridge Ministries
5554 North Federal Highway
Fort Lauderdale, Florida 33308
(305) 772-0404
Founder: Dr. D. James Kennedy

Dominion Press
7112 Burns Street
Fort Worth, Texas 76118
(800) 527-8608, (817) 284-1609 in Texas
Founder: Dr. Gary K. North

Eternal Word Television Network
5817 Old Leeds Road
Birmingham, Ala. 35210
(205) 956-5987
Founder: Mother Mary Angelica

Focus on the Family, Inc.
P.O. Box 500
Arcadia, California 91006
(818) 445-1579
President: James C. Dobson

Free Congress Political Action Committee
721 Second Street, NE.
Washington, D.C. 20002
(202) 546-3000
President: Richard Dingman

Free Congress Research and Education Foundation
721 Second Street, NE.
Washington, D.C. 20002
(202) 546-3004
President: Paul M. Weyrich

Institute for Christian Economics
P.O. Box 8000
Tyler, Texas 75711
President: Gary North, Ph.D.

In Touch Ministries
P.O. Box 7900
Atlanta, Georgia 30357
(404) 347-8300
Founder: Dr. Charles F. Stanley

James Robison Evangelistic Association
P.O. Box 18489
Fort Worth, Texas 76118
(817) 267-4211

Jimmy Swaggart Ministries
P.O. Box 2550
Baton Rouge, Louisiana 70821
(504) 769-8300
President: Jimmy Swaggart

Liberty Federation
717 Second Street, NE.
Washington, D.C. 20002
(202) 675-4040
President: Dr. Jerry C. Nims

Maranatha Christian Ministries
P.O. Box 1799
Gainsville, Florida 32602
(904) 375-6000
President: Robert Weiner

National Association of Evangelicals
P.O. Box 28
Wheaton, Illinois 60189
(312) 665-0500
President: Dr. Ray Hughes

National Committee of Catholic Laymen
150 East 35th Street
New York, New York 10157-0137
(212) 685-6666
Chairman: J. P. McFadden

National Jewish Coalition
415 Second Street, NE
Washington, D.C.
(202) 547-7701
National Chair: Richard J. Fox

National Pro-Family Coalition
721 Second Street, NE.
Washington, D.C. 20022
(202) 546-5342
Chairperson: Connaught Marshner

National Religious Broadcasters
CN 1926
Morristown, New Jersey 07960
(201) 428-5400
Executive Director: Dr. Ben Armstrong

Oral Roberts Evangelistic Association
P.O. Box 2187
Tulsa, Oklahoma 74101
(918) 495-6161
Founder: Dr. G. Oral Roberts

Radio Bible Class, Inc.
P.O. Box 22
Grand Rapids, Michigan 49555
(616) 942-6770
Chairman: Reverend Richard W. De Hann

Roundtable (The Religious)
P.O. Box 11467, 3295 Poplar Avenue
Memphis, Tennessee 38111
(901) 761-0512
President: Ed McAteer

Robert Schuller Ministries
Crystal Cathedral Communications
12141 Luis Street
Garden Grove, California 92640
(714) 971-4000
Founder: Dr. Robert H. Schuller

Summit Ministries
P.O. Box 207
Manitou Springs, Colorado 80829
(719) 685-9103
President: David A. Noebel

Thomas Aquinas College
10000 North Ojai Road
Santa Paula, California 93060
(805) 525-4417
President: Dr. Ronald McArthur

Tim LaHaye Ministries
Family Life Seminars
370 L'Enfant Promenade SW
Suite 801
Washington, D.C. 20024
(202) 488-0700
President: Dr. Tim LaHaye

Trinity Broadcasting Network
Box A
Santa Ana, California 92711
(714) 832-2950
President: Paul Crouch

BIBLIOGRAPHY

I. Primary source and reference materials on the Religious Right. Included in this are some works that focus primarily on conservatism in general or the secular right.

A. Books and pamphlets by or about fundamentalists and evangelicals whose views would justify categorizing them in the New Christian Right.

Armstrong, Ben. *The Electric Church.* Nashville: Thomas Nelson, 1979.

Billings, William. *The Christian's Political Action Manual.* Washington: National Christian Action Coalition, 1980.

Campbell, Ken. *No Small Stir: A Spiritual Strategy for Salting and Saving a Secular Society.* Burlington, Ont.: G. R. Welch, 1980.

Dobson, Edward. *Fundamentalism Today.* Chicago: Moody Press, 1984.

D'Souza, Dinesh. *Falwell Before the Millennium: A Critical Biography.* Chicago: Regnery Gateway, 1984.

Eidsmoe, John. *God and Caesar: Christian Faith and Political Action.* Westchester, IL: Crossway Books, 1984.

Falwell, Jerry. *Listen, America!* Garden City, NY: Doubleday, 1980.

———, ed., with Ed Dobson and Ed Hindson. *The Fundamentalist Phenomenon: The Resurgence of Conservative Christianity.* Garden City, NY: Doubleday, 1981.

Feulner, Edwin J., Jr. *Conservatives Stalk the House.* Ottawa, IL: Green Hill Publishers, 1983.

Howard, Donald R. *Rebirth of Our Nation: The Decline of the West 1970's—the Christian Educational Reform 1980's.* Accelerated Christian Education, Lewisville, TX 75067, 1979.

LaHaye, Tim. *The Battle for the Mind.* Old Tappan, NJ: Revell, 1980.

Nash, Ronald H. *Social Justice and the Christian Church.* Milford, MI: Mott Media, 1983.

Roberts, James C. *The Conservative Decade.* Westport, CT: Arlington House, 1980.

Robison, James with Jim Cox. *Save America to Save the World.* Wheaton, IL: Tyndale House, 1980.

Rothenberg, Stuart and Frank Newport. *The Evangelical Voter.* Washington: Free Congress Research and Educational Foundation, 1984.

Rusher, William A. *The Rise of the Right.* New York: Morrow, 1984.

Schaeffer, Francis A. *A Christian Manifesto.* Westchester, IL: Crossway Books, 1981.

———. *The Great Evangelical Disaster.* Westchester, IL: Crossway Books, 1984.

Schaeffer, Franky V. *Bad News for Modern Man: An Agenda for Christian Activism.* Westchester, IL: Crossway Books, 1984.

Schlafly, Phyllis. *The Power of the Christian Woman.* Cincinnati: Standard Publishing Co., 1981.

Strober, Gerald and Ruth Tomsczak McClellan. *The Jerry Falwell Story.* Ibex Publishing Co., 1203A O'Neill Hwy., Dunmore, PA 18512, 1982.

Walton, Rus. *FACS! Fundamentals for American Christians.* Marlborogh, NH: Plymouth Rock Foundation, 1979.

Whitaker, Robert W. *The New Right Papers.* New York: St. Martin's Press, 1982.

Whitehead, John W. *The Second American Revolution.* Elgin, IL: David C. Cook, 1982.

Willoughby, William. *Do We Need the Moral Majority?* Plainfield, NJ: Logos Haven Books, 1981.

B. Collections of primary source materials on the New Right and informational guides.

An American Dream: Neo-conservatism and New Religious Right in the USA. IDOC Bulletin (Via S. Maria dell'Anima 30, 00186 Rome, Italy), no. 8/9, 1982.

Anti-Defamation League of B'nai B'rith. *Extremism on the Right: A Handbook.* New York: ADL, 1983.

Michigan Education Association. *The New Right.* MEA, 1216 Kendale, East Lansing, MI 48823.

The New Right: Readings and Commentary. The Data Center, 464 19th St., Oakland, CA 94612, 1982.

Saperstein, Rabbi David, ed. *The Challenge of the Religious Right: A Jewish Response.* New York: Commission on Social Action of Reform Judaism, 1982.

Wilcox, Laird M. *Directory of the American Right.* Editorial Research Service, P.O. Box 1832, Kansas City, MO 64141.

C. Bibliographies of materials on conservatism and the New Christian Right.

Lazar, Ernie. *Bibliography on Conservative and Extreme Right Thought and Activity in the U.S. since 1960.* Privately published, 495 Ellis St., no. 1753, San Francisco, CA 94102, 1982, 1984.

Pierard, Richard V. *Bibliography on the New Christian Right.* Dept. of History, ISU, Terre Haute, IN 47809, 1981.

———. "The Christian Right: Suggestions for Further Reading," *Foundations* 25 (April-June 1982): 212 27.

———. "The New Religious Right: A Formidable Force in American Politics," *Choice* 19 (March 1982): 863-79.

———. "The New Religious Right in American Politics," in George Marsden, ed., *Evangelicalism and Modern America.* Grand Rapids: Eerdmans, 1984, pp. 161-74, 206-12.

Stackhouse, Max L. "Religious Right: New? Right?" *Commonweal* 109 (Jan. 24, 1982): 52-56.

Wilcox, Laird M. *The American Right: An Extensive Bibliography.* Editorial Research Service, P.O. Box 1832, Kansas City, MO 64141, regularly updated.

II. Selected secondary works and critiques of the New Right

Bell, Daniel, ed. *The Radical Right.* Garden City, NY: Doubleday, 1963.

Bollier, David. *Liberty and Justice for Some: Defending Free Society from the Radical Right's Holy War on Democracy.* New York: Frederick Ungar, 1983.

Bromley, David G. and Anson D. Shupe, eds. *New Christian Politics.* Macon, GA: Mercer University Press, 1984.

Conway, Flo and Jim Siegelman. *Holy Terror: The Fundamentalist War on America's Freedoms in Religion, Politics and Our Private Lives.* Garden City, NY: Doubleday, 1982.

Cooper, John Charles. *Religious Pied Pipers: A Critique of Radical Right Religion.* Valley Forge, PA: Judson Press, 1981.

Crawford, Alan. *Thunder on the Right: The "New Right" and the Politics of Resentment.* New York: Pantheon, 1980.

Dworkin, Andrea. *Right Wing Women: The Politics of Domesticated Females.* New York: Coward, McCann, 1983.

Ericson, Edward L. *American Freedom and the Radical Right.* New York: Frederick Ungar, 1982.

Fackre, Gabriel. *The Religious Right and the Christian Faith.* Grand Rapids: Eerdmans, 1982.

Finch, Philip. *God, Guts, and Guns: A Close Look at the Radical Right.* New York: Putnam, 1983.

Gross, Bertram. *Friendly Fascism: The New Face of Power in America.* New York: M. Evans, 1980.

Hadden, Jeffrey and Charles E. Swann. *Prime-time Preachers: The Rising Power of Televangelism.* Reading, MA: Addison-Wesley, 1981.

Hill, Samuel S. and Dennis E. Owen. *The New Religious- Political Right in America.* Nashville: Abingdon, 1982.

Johnson, George X. *Architects of Fear: Conspiracy Theories and Paranoia in American Politics.* Jeremy P. Tarcher, 9110 Sunset Blvd., Los Angeles, CA 90069, 1984.

Jorstad, Erling. *The Politics of Doomsday: Fundamentalists of the Far Right.* Nashville: Abingdon, 1970.

———. *The Politics of Moralism: The New Christian Right in American Life.* Minneapolis: Augsburg, 1981.

Kater, John L., Jr. *Christians on the Right: The Moral Majority in Perspective.* New York: Seabury, 1982.

Liebman, Robert C. and Robert Wuthnow. *The New Christian Right: Mobilization and Legitimation.* Hawthorne, NY: Aldine, 1983.

Maguire, Daniel. *The New Subversives: Anti-Americanism of the Religious Right.* New York: Continuum, 1982.

Miles, Michael. *The Odyssey of the American Right.* New York: Oxford University Press, 1980.

Neuhaus, Richard John. *The Naked Public Square: Religion and Democracy in America.* Grand Rapids: Eerdmans, 1984.

Noll, Mark A., Nathan O. Hatch, and George M. Marsden, eds. *The Search for Christian America.* Westchester, IL: Crossway Books, 1983.

Peele, Gillian. *Revival and Reaction: The Contemporary American Right.* Oxford: Oxford University Press, 1984.

Radi, Shirley L. *The Invisible Woman: The Hidden Agenda of the Religious New Right.* New York: Delacorte Press, 1983.

Shriver, Peggy L. *The Bible Vote: Religion and the New Right.* New York: Pilgrim Press, 1981.

Shupe, Anson and William Stacey. *Born Again Politics and the Moral Majority: What Social Surveys Really Show.* Lewisburg, NY: Edwin Mellen Press, 1982.

Singleton, James E., ed. *The Fundamentalist Phenomenon or Fundamentalist Betrayal: Leading Fundamentalists Speak Out.* Fundamental Baptist Press, 2150 E. Southern Ave., Tempe, AZ 85282, 1982.

———. *The Moral Majority: An Assessment of a Movement by Leading Fundamentalists.* Tempe, AZ: Fundamental Baptist Press, 1980.

Vetter, Herbert F., ed. *Speak Out Against the New Right.* Boston: Beacon Press, 1982.

Webber, Robert. *The Moral Majority—Right or Wrong?* Westchester, IL: Crossway Books, 1981.

Young, Perry Deane. *God's Bullies: Power Politics and Religious Tyranny.* New York: Holt, Rinehart, and Winston, 1982.

Zwier, Robert. *Born-Again Politics: The New Christian Right in America.* Downers Grove, IL: InterVarsity Press, 1982.

III. Substantial articles that analyze or critique the right from a scholarly perspective. Omitted are brief commentaries and newspaper articles as these are adequately cited in the bibliographies and secondary works.

Bennett, John C. "Assessing the Concerns of the Religious Right," *Christian Century* 98 (Oct. 14, 1981): 1018-22.

Blumenthal, Sidney. "The Righteous Empire," *New Republic* 46 (Oct. 22, 1984): 18-24.

Brown, Robert McAfee. "Listen, Jerry Falwell! A Response to Listen, America," *Christianity and Crisis* 40 (Dec. 22, 1980): 360-64.

Carey, George W. "Thunder on the Right: Lightning on the Left," *Modern Age* 25 (Spring 1981): 132-42.

Clouse, Robert G. "The New Christian Right, America, and the Kingdom of God," *Christian Scholar's Review* 12 (1983): 3-26.

Day-Lower, Donna. "Who Is the Moral Majority: A Composite Profile." *Union Seminary Quarterly Review,* 37 (1983): 335-49.

Denier, Greg. "A Shift Toward the Right? Or a Failure of the Left?" *Christianity and Crisis* 40 (Dec. 22, 1980): 355-60.

Dunn, James M. "Fanatical Fundamentalism and Political Extremism," *USA Today* 111 (May 1983): 53-55.

Ellerin, Milton and Alisa Kesten. "The New Right: What Is It?" *Social Policy* 11 (March-April 1981): 54-62.

FitzGerald, Frances. "A Reporter at Large: A Disciplined, Charging Army [Jerry Falwell]," *New Yorker* 57 (May 18, 1981): 53-141.

Gaffney, Edward McGlynn, Jr. "Biblical Religion and American Politics: Some Historical and Theological Reflections," *Journal of Law and Religion* 1 (Summer 1983): 171-86.

Gitlin, Todd. "When the Right Talks, TV Listens," *Nation* 239 (Oct. 15, 1983): 333-40.

Hadden, Jeffrey K. and Charles E. Swann. "Responding to the Christian Right," *Theology Today* 39 (Jan. 1983): 377-84.

Harrell, David Edwin, Jr. "The Roots of the Moral Majority: Fundamentalism Revisited," *Occasional Papers of the Institute for Ecumenical and Cultural Research* [Collegeville, MN 56321], No. 15, May 1981.

Hinson, E. Glenn. "Neo-Fundamentalism: An Interpretation and Critique," *Baptist History and Heritage* 16 (April 1981): 33-42.

Johnson, Stephen D. and Joseph B. Tamney. "The Christian Right and the 1980 Presidential Election," *Journal for the Scientific Study of Religion* 21 (June 1982): 123-31.

Linder, Robert D. "Militarism in Nazi Thought and in the Woof of the New American Religious Right," *Journal of Church and State* 24 (Spring 1982): 263-79.

Linesch, Michael. "Right-Wing Religion: Christian Conservatism as a Political Movement," *Political Science Quarterly* 97 (Fall 1982): 403-25

Marsden, George M. "Preachers of Paradox: The Religious New Right in Historical Perspective," in Mary Douglas and Steven M. Tipton, eds., *Religion and America: Spiritual Life in a Secular Age.* Boston: Beacon Press, 1983, pp. 150-68.

203

Marty, Martin E. "Morality, Ethics, and the New Christian Right," *Hastings Center Report*, Aug. 4, 1981, pp. 14-17.

North, Gary. "The Intellectual Schizophrenia of the New Christian Right." *Christianity and Civilization,* 1 (Spring 1982): 1-40.

Pierard, Richard V. "Evangelical Christianity and the Radical Right," in R. G. Clouse, R. D. Linder, R. V. Pierard, eds., *The Cross and the Flag.* Carol Stream, IL: Creation House, 1972, pp. 99-118.

―――. "The New Christian Right: A Threat to American Religious Freedom?" in Henry B. Clark II, ed., *Freedom of Religion in America.* New Brunswick, NJ: Transaction Books, 1982, pp. 89-98.

Rausch, David A. and Douglas E. Chismar. "The New Puritans and Their Theonomic Paradise," *Christian Century* 100 (Aug. 3-10, 1983): 712-15.

Ribuffo, Leo P. "Fundamentalism Revisited: Liberals and That Old-Time Religion," *Nation* 231 (Nov. 29, 1980): 570-73.

Rosenberg, Tina. "How the Media Made the Moral Majority," *Washington Monthly* 14 (May 1982): 26-34.

Shriver, Peggy L. "Piety, Pluralism, and Politics," in Ronald H. Stone, ed. *Reformed Faith and Politics.* Washington: University Press of America, 1983, pp. 49-63.

Wood, James E., Jr. "Religious Fundamentalism and the New Right," *Journal of Church and State* 22 (Autumn 1980): 409-21.

IV. All or a major part of these magazine issues were devoted to an assessment of the New Christian Right.

Christianity and Crisis, vol. 42, February 15, 1982.

engage/social action, vol. 2, January 1981.

Face to Face: An Interreligious Bulletin [Anti-Defamation League of B'nai B'rith], vol. 8, Winter 1981.

Foundations: A Baptist Journal of History, Theology, and Ministry, vol. 25, April-June 1982.

Light [Christian Life Commission of the Southern Baptist Convention], November 1980, March 1981, and July-August 1982.

Radical Religion, vol. 5, no. 4, 1981.

V. Books and Articles about Nuclear Armageddon Ideology

Efrid, James M. *End-Times: Rapture, Antichrist, Millenium.* Nashville: Abingdon Press, 1986.

Halsell, Grace. *Prophecy and Politics: Militant Evangelists on the Road to Nuclear War.* Westport, Conn.: Lawrence Hill, 1986.

Lang, Andrew G., and Clarkson, Fred. *Editors' and Reporters' Guide to the Religious Right.* Washington: The Christic Institute, 1987.

Scheer, Robert. "Rev. Jerry Falwell: The Prophet of 'Worldly Methods'." *Los Angeles Times,* 4 March 1985.

Lindsey, Hal. *The Late Great Planet Earth.* New York: Bantam Books, 1973.

Robertson, Pat. *The Secret Kingdom.* Nashville: Thomas Nelson, 1982.